Doctors gave Lareau Lindquist a 2% chance to live, but those odds changed when thousands of people prayed. Almighty God heard them and that adds the odds, from 2% to a 100% miracle!
John Pudaite
President, Bibles For The World

Lareau Lindquist got me interested in Missions during a trip to India. He is always a solid encourager. This book will encourage you and me to keep going when normal instincts tell us to quit.
Dennis Johnson
Author of Tell Me a Story and founder of Kids Around the World

We're bombarded with books of fictional anti-heroes and exposés of celebrities, but it's refreshing to read eyewitnesses' account of miracles that saved Lareau Lindquist's life.
Dr. Paul Larsen
Past President of Evangelical Covenant Church and Past President of North Park University.

LESS THAN TWO PERCENT CHANCE

LESS THAN TWO PERCENT CHANCE

A True Story about LIFE, DEATH,
and the POWER of PRAYER

Lareau Lindquist
& Evie Lindquist
with Joe Musser

Visit Lareau's website: www.barnabas.org
Less than Two Percent Chance – Lareau Lindquist
Copyright © 2016
First edition published 2016
All rights reserved. No part of this book may be reproduced, stored in a retrieval system, or transmitted in any form or by any means – electronic, mechanical, photocopying, recording, or otherwise, without written permission from the publisher.
Cover Design: Natalia Hawthorne, BookCoverLabs.com
eBook Icon: Icons Vector/Shutterstock
Editors: Joe Musser, Cheryl Warner, and Sheila Wilkinson

Printed in the United States of America
Aneko Press – *Our Readers Matter*™
www.anekopress.com
Aneko Press, Life Sentence Publishing, and our logos are trademarks of
Life Sentence Publishing, Inc.
203 E. Birch Street
P.O. Box 652
Abbotsford, WI 54405
BIOGRAPHY & AUTOBIOGRAPHY / Religious
Paperback ISBN: 978-1-62245-398-6
eBook ISBN: 978-1-62245-399-3

10 9 8 7 6 5 4 3 2 1
Available where books are sold

Contents

Dedication IX
Acknowledgments XI
Preface XIII
An Appointment with Death? 1
Facing the Grim Reaper 9
Evie: Recalling Lareau's First Hours 17
Getting the Doctors' Reports 23
Get the Word Out: Pray for Lareau! 29
Facing the Horror 37
Evie and a Heroic Angel 43
How Can You Replicate Someone's Face? 55
Evie's Encouragement 65
Lareau Awakens 73
Lareau's Dark Nights – Will God Retire Me? 79
My Mind and Body in Limbo 87
Concern from Around the World 97
The Paradox of Thorns 107
Thorns and Thrones 117
God Is the Healer 123
The Glory Factor 129
The Miracle Man 135
Is God Ever Too Late? 143
Photos 151
Lareau and Evie Lindquist Information 155
Meet the Author 157

Dedication

I dedicate my life and this book to the Lord. He took an ugly event and made something beautiful out of it. I can't imagine any person who can do that.

True, He used many individual humans. There were doctors, nurses, and others in healing careers (some who are identified in the Acknowledgements of this book). I may have missed others during my unconsciousness and coma. Nevertheless, God knows them and recognizes them.

Many, many people were at the crash site and helped save my life. It's a long list. I include them in the early narrative of the book. Other people's roles I discovered during my hospitalization. Each had a singular part to play, as did unknowing others during that first hour or so – first at the crash site, then an hour later at the ER.

Their singular action to save me was orchestrated by God in a series of events that had taken place in a split-second sequence. Only God can do that. Yet I do recognize those people on the site who helped.

I also recognize the many doctors, nurses, and assistants who were available that night when the ER called for help. That too was orchestrated by God.

Throughout those emergencies, God was the Master Healer, supervising the work that had to be done. I am reminded of a physician I met in India who gave me his business card that said, "I Practice Medicine; God Heals People."

Others that I may have missed in this dedication, I am grateful to them nonetheless.

Johann Sebastian Bach was a remarkable, great musician. Bach penned the initial letters *SDG* for the phrase in Latin, *Soli Deo Gloria,* on sheets of his magnificent sacred music. In English it translates: *To the Glory of God Alone.* Billy Graham wrote similar words at the end of his autobiography. With sincere humility, I join with these great men in saying: TO GOD BE THE GLORY.

Acknowledgments

Evie, my wife, was with me throughout my ordeal. She was my constant strength and encouragement during my hospitalization and recovery. Evie and I co-authored this book.

Joe Musser, with whom I've done several other books, was also co-author and involved in every aspect of this book.

Cheryl Warner served as the copy editor, reviewing the finished manuscript and helping create a smooth, readable book.

Staff members of Barnabas International became involved on the night of my accident. They were constant partners offering encouragement and prayerful support through the long weeks in the hospital.

My four children and eight grandchildren accepted my ordeal with grace. They tasted some of the pain that extended from days, then into weeks and months. Their love and prayers sustained me.

And those who had experienced their own catastrophic accidents inspired me during my difficult journey: Joni Eareckson

Tada (*Joni* and her many other books), Jerry Sittser (*A Grace Disguised*), and Don Piper (*90 Minutes in Heaven*). Their accidents, subsequent life changes, and their books inspired me – both before my accident and more since my accident. I've known them from a distance but their experiences and encouragements have significantly had an impact on me.

I am grateful also to many doctors, nurses, and hospital staff members (St. Anthony Hospital in Rockford, Illinois) who contributed to my healing.

Finally, I want to acknowledge the hundreds of friends (known and unknown to me) from all over the world, who prayed for me then, and some still pray now. To this day I hear from many of them.

Preface

This is my story of the frightful night of Friday, January 22, 1999. Yet, it's because of memories and accounts of others that my story has gone around the world – from person to person, prayer chain to prayer chain, church to church, and country to country.

Today, sixteen years after a night far removed with time, events of that night continue in my thoughts and memories.

Friends, family members, and even strangers were all somehow involved in that event. They contributed to my story through their accounts of that night, making it their story as well.

For two weeks in January 1999, I ministered in Kenya for mission organizations and churches in that nation. For years I'd been making trips all over the world through Barnabas International, the organization that my wife, Evie, and I founded in 1986.

When I finished two weeks in Kenya, I boarded a plane in Nairobi and started my return trip to the United States – first from Nairobi to London, where I changed planes. Then I flew from London to Chicago's O'Hare International Airport. After the two flights, I took the airport bus from O'Hare to Rockford, Illinois.

This final 8,600-mile trip crossed hemispheres to end my trip home. With only five miles more to complete my long, long journey, I was grateful for God's protection, crossing thirteen time zones and traveling from half a world away.

I was really tired from 30-plus hours in transit and changing planes, but I was a United Two-Million-Mile flier and was used to long-distance travel.

I'd already learned that transition from one continent to another can be difficult. When traveling halfway around the world, changing time zones confuses your body clock and leaves you exhausted with jet lag.

I was one of those people who tried to master time zones. When I got to my destinations, I tried to adjust to the local time and usually didn't have complications. I know many people have to spend days trying to get in sync for an overseas destination or getting confused again when they return to their home country.

After a decade or more of globetrotting for Barnabas International, I adapted by napping on planes or in airport lounges, but they aren't like my own bed in Rockford. I was able to handle the latter leg of the flights, but January 22, 1999, at a short four-to-five-mile car trip to my home, I nearly died. That's the story of this book.

In writing this story, my collaborator-author Joe Musser, Evie, and I have researched the details of what transpired Friday, January 22, 1999, when I was in a collision that nearly took my life.

PREFACE

The title of the book gives the raw and scary prospect that a doctor shared with Evie while other doctors and surgeons were working on me in the emergency room: "Mrs. Lindquist, I'm sorry... but your husband has critical injuries from the crash. He has only a two percent chance of living through the night."

It was a terrible night. Yet miraculously I *did* live through that night, and the days and nights to follow, but they were starkly fearful.

Those somber details from the doctors set the stage for some terrible times. Of course, for the days following my accident, I was in a coma and didn't know how badly I was injured. My family had to bear what was to transpire with the cadre of surgeons for orthopedics, internal exams, ophthalmological exams and repairs, plastic surgery, teeth and jaw reconstruction. Other teams consisted of technicians: for X-rays, MRIs, brain scans, blood plasma and other transfusions, as well as the platoons of nurses and technicians attending to catheters, tubes, wires, restraints, and monitors.

Fortunately for me, I was in a coma while doctors worked to keep me alive. Because I was "out of it" for quite a while, I have only snatches of memories, and even some of those "memories" might have been dreams or hallucinations induced by the medications that were pumped into me to curb the intense pain.

The details for this story come from interviews with friends, family members, medical personnel, and even people we never met. There were accounts by those who happened to come on the scene of the car crash incident that is the focus of this book.

Some accounts are from newspaper articles and TV features. Scores of letters and cards, emails, photographs, and reports were sent to us to give this book an accurate and detailed account, not just of the incident on that January night but what took place in far-flung places as the news circled the globe.

Literally thousands of people in Nairobi, Kenya, Africa; Sielmat-Churachandpur, Manipur, India; scattered sites and cities in South America; Austria, Europe; places in the Far East; and scores of cities in America were prompted to pray for me, and the most remarkable miracles transpired as a result.

Inspiring aspects of the story will surprise many of our friends that we've never had an opportunity to share with until now.

With gratefulness to God for His protection and love, I trust you'll see that miracles not only occurred in Bible times, but God graciously provides them today.

More than anything else, the lesson I learned from this experience was that God's promises are not just theoretical – they are personal. We're not taught to simply trust in God's promises; we must *trust in God Himself*, just as the apostle Peter said in his epistle:

> *I know, even though you are temporarily harassed by all kinds of trials and temptations. This is no accident – it happens to prove your faith, which is infinitely more valuable than gold, and gold, as you know, even though it is ultimately perishable, must be purified by fire. This proving of your faith is planned to bring you praise and honour and glory in the day when Jesus Christ reveals himself.*
> 1 Peter 1:6-7

—Lareau Lindquist Rockford, Illinois

Chapter One

An Appointment with Death?

I knew I was cutting it close. My trip to Africa for two weeks of ministry was completed, and I had less than forty-eight hours for the journey home to Rockford, Illinois.

I had to be there in time to officiate at a wedding – a special wedding. I was to perform the marriage ceremony of my youngest daughter, Michelle, and her fiancé, James.

Fortunately I had no travel delays getting home on time, even though the trip took thirty-six hours of chasing the western horizon across thirteen time zones.

The nuptials began on time in the Fireside Room of the First Evangelical Free Church of Rockford (where I formerly had been pastor). Michelle and James beamed as the ceremony proceeded, and they kissed as I pronounced them man and wife.

The bridal party and friends went to Giovanni's Restaurant for the bridal dinner. As everyone was being seated, I told my wife, Evie, that I was totally "whipped" by fatigue and the effects of my long trip.

"I'm more tired than hungry," I said to Evie. "I'll take my car, stop at the office to pick up my mail, and go home."

I went outside where the cold January wind kept me alert and eager to get home and to the warm bed awaiting me. I got in my Pontiac Sunbird and headed for East State Street, where I turned right toward my office about a mile away.

What happened next is a studied reconstruction of facts and events pieced together by my office staff and witnesses or bystanders who were at the site that I'd reach within minutes.

Dottie Campbell (office manager of Barnabas International, where my office was located) recalled later that evening that I told her I'd pick up the mail on my way home, but it was apparent that I didn't stop by the office that night. Whether that would have made a difference, who knows? I often wonder.

After leaving the parking lot and heading for East State Street, I have no recollection about what happened next. However, friends, police reports, and eyewitnesses have given me an almost moment-by-moment account of my time that night.

Bob Ellison is a member of First Evangelical Free Church in Rockford, and he knew me. At the time, he was a freelance reporter for WTVO television station in Rockford. That night Bob was listening to a police and fire department radio scanner and heard the news about a crash on Alpine Road, so he drove to the collision site and followed the events from the chatter between the first responders. He came upon the scene and took notes on everything he saw.

Others were also interviewed. They recalled the events vividly and helped us lay out a timeline of where I was during that time and what took place.

AN APPOINTMENT WITH DEATH?

* * *

Friday, January 22, 1999

Approx. 8:35 p.m. – My Pontiac Sunbird went west on East State Street and moments later passed Mulford Road, going toward Phelps Avenue, where I didn't turn toward my office. I kept going west toward Alpine Road.

8:40 p.m. – Kristin Dolphin was sitting in her car in the driveway of her home on Warren Avenue, a mile east of Alpine Road where my car would "rendezvous" only moments later and where she would become a hero.

Kristin and her husband, Jeff, were taking Kristin's friend Rita Versendaal home. Jeff finally backed the car out of the driveway, and they headed east on Guilford toward Alpine.

8:41 p.m. – On East State Street my Sunbird turned right on Alpine Road, headed north toward the intersection of Alpine and Spring Creek Road, where I usually turned to go home. The Sunbird was still two miles from Spring Creek Road, about three miles to my home.

8:42 p.m. – Bill Levitt and his wife, Sue, were also on their way home, heading south on Alpine Road. He stopped for a red light at the intersection of Alpine and Brendenwood Roads. He recalls that the light stayed red longer than usual. "It seemed several minutes for the light to turn from red to green," he said later.

LESS THAN TWO PERCENT CHANCE

8:43 p.m. – The Pontiac Sunbird passed Aldeen Park, continuing north on Alpine, passing side streets of Rural, Guilford, and Abbotsford. As it was a typical Friday night with busy traffic in all lanes of Alpine, there was no reason yet to notice the Sunbird heading north.

8:44 p.m. – Then there was an empty space in the southbound lanes, where traffic waited for the long red light at Brendenwood Road and Alpine. Bill Levitt, waiting for the light to turn, saw it finally change. He pulled away in response to the now-green traffic light.

8:45:05 p.m. – I apparently fell asleep at the wheel, oblivious of that oncoming vehicle. My two-door Sunbird drifted across oncoming lanes at a speed that was estimated between 35 to 50 mph.

8:45:10 p.m. – Bill Levitt started moving south when the light turned green. He saw my car coming his way and braked to avoid hitting the Sunbird, which took a northwest trajectory, crossing the southbound lanes toward a nearby yard. Bill instinctively knew that if the red light hadn't held him back for those seconds, he would've been hit by the careening Sunbird.

8:45:11 p.m. – Other cars in all the Alpine lanes reacted instantly to avoid the crash. No cars were hit.

Meanwhile my Pontiac raced in that northwest trajectory across the four-lane highway without hitting other cars – yet directly toward a nearby stand of pine trees. Some small thinner

AN APPOINTMENT WITH DEATH?

evergreens acted as a screen for the muffling traffic noise, but there were also mature evergreens, one of which was in the path of my car.

8:45:12 p.m. – Packed, icy snow had been piled at the curb by an earlier snowplow that pushed the snow from the highway onto the curbs and people's yards. The ice-covered snow on the curbs was at least two feet high with a slight sloping angle. That crusty plowed snow suddenly turned the curb into a ramp.

8:45:13 p.m. – My Pontiac Sunbird hit the "ski ramp" and became airborne, hanging in the air for a millisecond, then came to a violent, explosive stop against a two-foot-circumference pine tree. The Sunbird slammed against it five feet above the ground.

Within milliseconds, my body inside the Sunbird went through the physics of inertia, and I instantly experienced a violent reaction to the collision. I can't remember if I was wearing my seat belt, but either way the inertial force of the collision caused immediate, relentless damage to my body.

My body was lifted up by inertia from the driver's seat and sent forward. My chest slammed against the steering wheel that simultaneously pinned my legs underneath its post.

That action resulted in instant rib and skull fractures and facial lacerations. Blood from facial cuts trickled onto my dark suit and topcoat.

8:45:20 p.m. – A stunned witness to the crash quickly pulled his car over to the curb and called 911. The 911 operator forwarded the report of the accident to the Rockford Fire Department station on Rural Street, west of Fairview, and the alarm for Engine 10.

8:47:24 p.m. – Two minutes later Bob Ellison saw the wreck as he turned his GMC pickup from Alpine Road onto Alpine Court, a short cul-de-sac about sixty feet from where my car crashed. He was only blocks away when his police scanner picked up the first responses who immediately received them after the 911 call.

Bob quickly used his cell phone to call the news desk of WTVO to get a TV crew to the site before the ambulance left the scene with a victim. His scanner got him to emergencies, and he knew many of the first responders, including fire department's Engine 10 of Rockford, were already heading toward the crash. Ironically Bob got there before them.

8:48:30 p.m. – Jeff Dolphin turned his vehicle from Guilford onto North Alpine Road. Seeing the crash, he pulled into Alpine Court and parked. He rushed from his car, leaving his wife Kristin and the baby with her friend Rita to wait.

Jeff saw the chaos near Alpine Court. After trotting over to the wreckage, he got a look at the helpless driver of the Sunbird and saw what he thought was a man with terrible injuries.

Jeff waved to Kristin, who was still in the car, to come; she was a cardiac nurse and might be able to assist any crash victims. Kristin hurried over to the accident scene while her friend Rita stayed in the car with the baby.

Reaching the wrecked car, Kristin saw the driver's side

window was rolled down halfway. She reached inside to see if the driver was breathing and if he had a pulse.

He *was* both breathing and had a pulse – but barely. Kristin saw Bill Levitt nearby and said, "I'm a nurse. I'll call this in to 911. Will you keep an eye on the victim? If he stops breathing, let me know."

Bill tried to rouse the victim by leaning toward the driver's open window, encouraging him. "Hey, man. You've gotta keep breathing! C'mon, take a deep breath, okay? Keep breathing."

Kristin gave vital information to a 911 operator, describing the victim's serious injuries and said, "We need an ambulance and paramedics sent to the corner of Alpine Road and Alpine Court."

Meanwhile Jeff Dolphin trotted over to Alpine Road and directed traffic on the highway, waving cars away from the scene until the police could get there.

Chapter Two

Facing the Grim Reaper

For many weeks, I didn't know how close to death I was. I should've died at the scene, but I didn't. I was saved by the grace of God and the number of people at the site who offered their help and first responder skills and assistance, while other passersby at the crash site offered prayers for my situation.

According to the accident report, my car swerved across Alpine Road and slammed into a tree. Only five minutes after the crash, a small cluster of bystanders gathered to see what was going on.

At the same time, some on site had medical and other skills, and they immediately started attending to my injuries and trying to keep me alive until the first responders came on the scene. People like Kristin and Jeff Dolphin and Bob Ellison were active at the scene even before the arrival of the police, fire department, and ambulance EMTs.

There was more taking place at the scene of the accident site.

Other reports turned up later, the next day. There was more than the police accident report; individual interviews would later filter into other blanks because the people at the site were offering help before the fire, police, and ambulance.

Including the first critical hour at the crash site that took place in the chronology listed in Chapter One, there was another dimension that took place.

* * *

Bob Ellison felt the impulse to pray for the victim (me) trapped in the wrecked car. Bob knew me but didn't recognize me because of my injuries, and he was overshadowed by his earlier experiences of other events.

Ironically, Bob's hobby of listening to police and fire departments on his scanner had both good and bad considerations. Earlier that day he went to two first-responder incidents – one for a man who lived not far away from Alpine Road, who had collapsed with a heart attack while shoveling snow.

Bob recalled that after EMTs gave CPR to the heart attack victim earlier that day, the ambulance took the man to Swedes, a nickname for Swedish-American Hospital. That's when Bob silently prayed for the snow-shoveling man to survive his heart attack.

Another incident occurred later in the day when an auto accident victim was trapped in his car. The Blackhawk Fire Department was dispatched to the site of the wreck. They tried to rescue the driver but without success. The man trapped in his car died. Bob had prayed for him too, but he also died.

So now, at the Alpine Road crash site, Bob didn't know if he should pray for the man in this car wreck. He could see he had many injuries. Recalling his other two victims he prayed for, he guessed that this victim's injuries were likely fatal.

Bob struggled with the fact that those other men didn't survive in spite of his prayers. As he wrestled with his heart whether it was even practical to pray for me, he had a feeling that it was probably too late for me.

Bob thought, *I don't recognize this guy. He looks like he's dead – or shortly will be. Poor guy won't make it.*

* * *

Meanwhile Kristin Dolphin was using the skills of her critical, cardiac nurse training, trying to help the trapped injured motorist in the Sunbird. She crawled into the crumpled front seat by way of the open window on the passenger side of the car. Finding no pulse, she immediately started chest compressions to keep her patient's blood circulating. Then she began CPR. For several minutes, she continued the methodical pounding of my chest.

She knew if she let up or didn't keep my heart and lungs functioning, I'd probably not make it. Without her CPR, I would have died at the crash site.

Then several police cars appeared at the scene. Two officers took over directing traffic from Jeff Dolphin, sending the cars into single lanes on both directions on Alpine, clearing space for emergency crews to approach and depart.

Two other police officers began investigating the crash. They walked the path of the Sunbird's tracks through the snow and gauged the angles of the vehicle's tracks. An angular, snowy path from across the street marked the driver's trajectory. It appeared there was no braking; no skid marks were on the dry concrete road. That meant the driver didn't stop or try to gain control.

The police also assumed that the driver likely fell asleep at the wheel or was driving under the influence of alcohol, yet the nurse and paramedics detected no liquor on the driver's breath or inside the car.

Kristin kept up with the chest compressions for the cardiopulmonary resuscitation. It's what keeps the heart beating, but when I stopped breathing, Kristin began to give me mouth-to-mouth resuscitation as well.

A fire department paramedic team inside an emergency fire truck was racing through traffic, its siren screaming, arriving at the accident scene not quite six minutes after the crash occurred.

Immediately on arrival the paramedics unloaded their gear and hurried to the Sunbird, where they saw that the driver was pinned inside and had major injuries. They first guided an oxygen tank into the open passenger window, so Kristin could adjust it to feed lifesaving oxygen into the victim's lungs. Her CPR compressions had kept my heart beating, and the oxygen tank continued my breathing.

The paramedics saw the predicament of a tall man (six feet, four inches) crumbled under the dashboard and steering wheel. An EMT climbed in the same window that Kristin had, though it was cramped with her, the EMT, and the victim inside on the small front seat.

The EMT eventually pulled himself into what was left of

that part of the car. He called to the other EMT outside the car. "The driver's seat is jammed against the back seat. I can't get leverage to get him out."

There was a quick decision to use the Jaws of Life, which requires a power saw to cut away parts of the car to get the victim out of the wreck and into an ambulance – but it was still on its way.

Kristin took charge before the fire department came, and when it did arrive, she thanked God for the firemen on site who got an oxygen unit inside the car, so the victim could breathe. Kristin also convinced the paramedics not to use the Jaws of Life.

"It's too dangerous," she told them. "He's barely breathing, and he's bleeding. Cutting him out of the car will take too much time. We have to get him out from under the dashboard where he's pinned and lift him out through a window. It's too dangerous any other way. Please! Help me lift him out of the car."

The paramedics agreed, deferring to Kristin's suggestions. Then the ambulance arrived with more helpers, who hurried over to the paramedics and Kristin.

For ten minutes they all wrestled to rescue the victim inside the crushed auto – to carefully twist and tease his long frame out from under the dashboard, firewall, and steering post. With cautious attention to pinned-down legs and pelvis, they finally got me out, still unconscious and critical.

The paramedics and Kristin lifted the unconscious victim hand over hand, through the car's passenger window and onto a gurney. The ambulance medics then slid the gurney into the back of the ambulance and started to check for other injuries.

LESS THAN TWO PERCENT CHANCE

* * *

Bob Ellison mentioned to a bystander, "I saw two guys die today. WTVO reported their deaths on the five o'clock news. Looks like another fatality might happen here." Bob arched his thumb over his shoulder, pointing toward the wreck.

Then, from his portable scanner Bob heard a fireman calling ahead to the hospital. "Hot loading to St. Anthony."[1]

Bob explained the radio jargon to a bystander: "He's saying it's not good – the victim has life-threatening injuries. They can't do much for him, but it's only about two miles to St. Anthony Hospital."

Bob watched as two EMTs climbed into their ambulance behind the stretcher and closed the doors as the vehicle sped away with its siren blaring. About the same time, a flatbed truck pulled up to haul away the totally wrecked Sunbird.

As Bob wondered if he should pray that God would save the life of the victim, reminding himself that, after all, when he prayed earlier, both men died from their injuries. *Is this one too late also?*

Bob witnessed a number of accident sites over his years of covering accidents, and after seeing the man put into the ambulance, Bob believed that this victim wasn't going to live much longer. His injuries were obviously fatal. Bob continued wrestling with those thoughts, as he left the crash site and drove a few blocks to where he lived – only moments from the accident.

Once home, Bob turned off the engine and sat quietly with

---

1   The hospital name, known in earlier years as St. Anthony Hospital, more recently was changed to the present official name, OSF (which is an abbreviation of Order of Saint Francis).

his hands still on the steering wheel. Before getting out of his GMC, he paused to pray for the man he'd just seen taken away at the collision site. He asked God to spare the life of the man, despite his apparent fatal injuries.

* * *

Meanwhile, back at the crash site, Kristin walked slowly back to their car, where Jeff, their baby, and Rita were waiting. She was physically exhausted from all that had taken place over the past half hour. Adrenalin had energized her actions, enabling her to keep my heart beating and my lungs breathing.

Her mind was still racing: *Will our help be enough to keep that man alive until they even get him to the hospital?*

"I wonder who he was," Kristin said aloud to herself as she got into her car. She didn't notice that she spoke in the past tense, as if *I might already be dead.*

* * *

Bill Levitt, Bob Ellison, and Kristin Dolphin had no idea that *I* was the person in the crash. Even people who knew me wouldn't have recognized me.

Later, when the newspaper and TV news videos reported my accident, Mervyl Skillings saw the television news clip of the crash. She looked at the wrecked Sunbird displayed on the TV and said to her husband, Otis, "That car looks like Lareau's." Yet neither Mervyl nor Otis had any clue that it *was* my car. They would hear the information the next day, when phone calls from Barnabas staff members reported the accident and asked for prayers for my survival and recovery.

Four of those who were at the scene – Kristin Dolphin, Bob Ellison, and Bill and Sue Levitt – would also be stunned that they gave encouragement and helped to keep me alive. Others also prayed for God to save my life, but at the time, none of those people had any idea I was the victim, a Rockford pastor all four of them knew well. Ironically, for Bob Ellison, I was even his former pastor.

In the case of Kristin Dolphin, she was a cardiac nurse in the hospital where I'd been taken, where my wife, Evie, was also a nurse. They were nurses who worked on different floors, yet the two women knew each other. They would find out only days later that I had been kept alive in the crash by Evie's hospital coworker Kristin Dolphin who surely did save my life at the scene.

Chapter Three

Evie: Recalling Lareau's First Hours

My first knowledge that my husband, Lareau, had been in a horrific automobile accident was when the hospital chaplain phoned me. We had just returned home from the wedding dinner at Giovanni's Restaurant. I thought Lareau had stopped at his office as he said he would, so I wasn't surprised that we didn't find him at home when we returned.

The hospital chaplain told me that Lareau was in a serious accident in his car and was still in the ER where doctors were attending to his injuries. However, the chaplain didn't get into the nature of his injuries or his condition. He merely said, "Mrs. Lindquist, the ER doctors are attending to your husband. You might want to come to the hospital."

The news was a shock. *Lareau? In the hospital? An accident?* A shudder made me shiver as I hung up the phone. I had more questions than answers about Lareau's accident, but as a nurse, I knew chaplains are not given medical information about the patients.

Fortunately, just thirty seconds later the chaplain phoned me back.

"Mrs. Lindquist, I should have added that it'd be a good idea for you to *come right away*. The doctors didn't given me any details, but I sense they feel that your husband's condition is urgent. You should come right away."

I was stunned.

We'd just gotten home from the restaurant, and (except for the bride and groom) our other children and the grandchildren were with me. They all sensed something was wrong.

There was a moment of confusion and questions, but then we immediately decided to drive to the hospital, less than ten minutes away. My son Reese drove me, and my son Jeff and daughter Jodi also came. I was glad Jeff, a physician himself, was with us. I hoped he'd have some knowledge of Lareau's injuries.

We both knew it must be serious if the chaplain emphasized, "Your husband has been in a car accident," and "please, come *right away*."

In any typical hospital emergency room, it's generally a scene of managed chaos. At times several doctors might be involved with a critical patient.

I learned only later that with Lareau's situation, the ER team was ready to examine and treat him as soon as the ambulance brought him in. They had been apprised of his condition by the emergency crew at the scene of the wreck, the 911 operator, and a cardiac nurse who came to the crash site even before the first responders.

EVIE: RECALLING LAREAU'S FIRST HOURS

That young nurse had discovered some problems with Lareau at the crash site and passed her findings ahead to the ER doctors to anticipate the injuries. These "heads-up" reports provided the hospital with critical information on the kind of trauma and injuries the victim in the wreck might have sustained. However, I was not yet given this data.

Anticipating the worst and hoping for the best, the emergency room doctor and nurses try their best to determine the most serious injuries, doing triage well into the night. I knew what takes place in the ER, having spent years as a nurse, and now, with Lareau in the emergency room, I was grateful for the lifesaving attention of those doctors and nurses.

When Jeff and I got to the hospital ER area, we were greeted by the chaplain and Dr. Mark Soriano. Dr. Soriano knew me as one of the hospital's nurses, and I introduced my son Jeff to him.

He told me that the entire ER team had been working on Lareau for hours, making emergency repairs on his critical injuries, which would require more sophisticated surgeries when Lareau was stable enough to tolerate them.

"Your husband has received X-rays, CAT scans, and MRIs. The CAT scans recorded positive indications of brain activity, which means the scans of that part of the brain show he's still alive."

I looked at the doctor's expression; his eyes and face showed deep concern. I asked him, "Yes, I get that. Lareau is still alive . . . but *what*?"

Dr. Soriano was trying to say the right words to lift the family's spirits, but as a physician, he also had to let us know the blunt details as well. He ticked off the most serious of Lareau's injuries, and he tried to convey to us the most logical outcome of his injuries.

He explained that Lareau's body had absorbed several kinds of trauma from the collision, and the fact that his heart and brain were still functioning despite all his injuries indicated positive outcomes.

Yet the doctor didn't present a prognosis, neither positive nor negative. Instead he spoke to us in more technical medical terms than he would for typical family members who aren't familiar with the terms and who are often overwhelmed by the words and procedures described by doctors and nurses.

I took moments to absorb the doctor's report, glad that Jeff and I knew the terminology. We both understood the medical jargon; it was that jargon that was saving my husband's life and keeping him alive (though barely).

What Dr. Soriano was telling me about Lareau's brain activity was positive news, but I sensed a hesitation in his voice, as if he was holding back critical information.

There are times when doctors do hold back such consequential news, usually it's because various situations can have an undetermined outcome. They can go either way. Such unknowns also reduce confidence in the patient's outcome. Why tell them the bad news if no one knows that it's a 50/50 chance of life or death?

I think I perceived that hesitation in the doctor's explanation, but I let it go for the time being. A bit later another doctor came into the area outside the emergency room. I asked him, "I understand my husband's still alive. Thank God, doctor, but…?"

I stopped to look into his eyes. His face seemed grim. So I added, "That he's alive is the good news. How *bad* is it?"

The doctor averted his eyes for an instant.

I pressed him. "Please, Doctor, we have to know *what you know.*"

"It's bad, Mrs. Lindquist, really bad."

"Can we see him?"

The doctor nodded and escorted Jeff and me into the Intensive Care Unit. Despite my years of nursing experience in such trauma incidents, I gasped aloud.

I wasn't ready to see *my husband* in such a terrible situation. His face was so battered and swollen that I didn't even recognize him. His chest was also swollen and tightly bandaged. I only recognized his hands as being his.

I put my hand on his and stroked his fingers softly. *I thought I felt a response, and my heart skipped a beat.*

However, there was no other perceptible movement. I felt *something* – something that encouraged me as I stood there staring at the wounded man in the hospital bed.

Another doctor and the chaplain escorted us out of the ICU after just a few minutes with Lareau.

"Can't you give us any encouragement about his prognosis?" Jeff asked the other doctor when we were in the hall.

"You two already know more than ordinary family members who ask the doctor for information. You know that when there's no sure outcome one way or the other, we don't usually tell them what *might* happen. We don't speculate on life or death considerations. As you know, they could go either way," he said.

"I know that," I said. "Just tell me what your gut instincts tell *you* – based on Lareau's injuries and the probable results of his trauma. What do *you* say about his chances?"

At first the doctor was reluctant, but then he said, "The ER doctors and surgeons say that there's only a two percent chance that he'll live through the night."

His words were kind and soft, without inflection, and tempered with compassion – as if he was trying to avoid words too harsh and weighty for us to accept.

However, his words carried weight – words that had authority and wisdom, warning us what to expect over the next hours.

The doctor's words, *There's only a two percent chance that he'll live through the night.* The doctor's voice had great seriousness and fearful importance.

Neither Jeff nor I said anything as we walked toward the visitors' waiting room. Our thoughts were racing after hearing that stark report. Neither of us knew what to do next. We were so stunned and confused that we didn't even know what to pray for, except for Lareau to live.

The doctor's words made me shudder, *There's only a two percent chance that he'll live through the night.*

Chapter Four

Getting the Doctors' Reports

The warning that Lareau was likely to die sometime during the early morning hours struck us as a death sentence. Although it wasn't intended to crush all hope, it certainly had that result.

My head was spinning. How could it be? Would we part so soon, without good-byes and not knowing what had happened to Lareau? The car crashed into a tree large enough to have killed Lareau instantly, but he was still alive when he was brought to the hospital.

Could that mean that he won't die? Is God going to intervene for Lareau? Or will he go to heaven within the next few hours?

Thoughts and fragments of information all tumbled in my brain. I had to close my eyes and try to visualize what my husband had been doing on his way home. And more to the point at that moment, what was he going through now?

The doctors and nurses had completed the emergency

treatment, helping him breathe with a tracheal tube, stopping his bleeding, cleaning the wounds, and stabilizing his broken bones. There were obviously many more things that took place before taking him to the ICU, but they couldn't give any long-term attention to the broken bones, destroyed facial muscles, and skin.

Inside my head I kept hearing the doctor's words, *There's only a two percent chance that he'll live through the night.* It was a statement of finality.

The reports of other doctors would tell what they had done to save Lareau's life and how they did their best to prevent any further danger. That information would be recorded afterward and put into the hospital system for transcribing, but we wouldn't see the medical transcripts immediately.

During the initial consultation about Lareau's condition was when they made their dire evaluations, but we weren't always provided with that information. Because we weren't given the actual reports of Lareau's doctors, we didn't know what was going on in the process, and I was frustrated.

However, as a nurse in the hospital, I knew that the doctor's notes were carefully held back for the patient's protection and privacy. It was the proper way to handle it. Still, it frustrated me not having all the information the doctors had. Not knowing meant it took a long time for us to get any little news that was positive.

Seeing how Lareau looked that night made it easy to believe that the doctors' two percent chance was accurate. In similar situations, it was not unusual to have many specialists examining the victim brought in with terrible trauma. Time was of the essence. Typically, many lives are lost because of trauma that involves too many injuries, treatment that is late, or complications that arise.

With Lareau, a diverse staff of more than a dozen medical personnel were called in to consult, and they contributed to the initial exams. Emergency room doctors – surgeons, anesthesiologists, radiologists, pulmonologists, neurologists, ophthalmologists, oral surgeons, plastic surgeons, orthopedic surgeons, internists, and others – were called into action over the first hours, then days.

It would have been far less stressful for us if we could have seen the doctors' reports of Lareau's treatment and outcomes on that fateful night. But we only got those reports long after that night when many medical specialists worked on him in the ER and then in the ICU.

When we began writing this book, we were finally able to get copies of the original hospital reports that related to Lareau's treatment. Those reports helped us to shape the chronology of the events of that night and the following days, weeks, and months that Lareau was in the hospital and a rehabilitation center.

The reports were in chronological order. The very first reports were to the point: "A sixty-two-year-old gentleman driver of a motor vehicle who either fell asleep or lost control of his vehicle, ran off the road, and struck a tree, and first exams [showed that he] suffered a concussion, intracerebral hemorrhage, and multiple facial fractures."

Lareau was brought into the hospital at about 9:30 the night of January 22, 1999. Three and a half hours later, during the early hours of January 23, a surgeon was brought in to assess the "multiple blunt trauma" which included all three of the previous pre-op diagnoses.

A different doctor supervised a portable chest X-ray to compare with the CAT scan of Lareau's head by another doctor on duty who set up the CAT scan, mainly a scan of Lareau's brain to see if he had a hemorrhage inside his head.

An observation from the CAT scan indicated that an MRI was required for a more sensitive image with more details of problem areas.

That doctor's report said, "There is an undiagnosed lesion in the CAT scan of the brain. This raises the possibility perhaps of seizure," which required the MRI. "A seizure could have triggered the event" that caused Lareau to run off the road.

We later learned that this was not the case; there was no lesion on Lareau's brain, and neither was a seizure detected.

Another treatment made use of an endotracheal tube. It is inserted into the trachea to serve as a passage through the upper airway. In this case, the doctor noted, "The patient has been hemodynamically stable," meaning that the bleeding in Lareau's lungs stopped.

The endotracheal tube was also a device to suction out the bloody secretions in his lungs, probably a result of the "blunt trauma" in his chest. He also reported that the patient "has marked facial swelling with abrasions, lacerations." He added, "The patient is intubated on mechanical ventilation," meaning that Lareau wasn't capable of breathing on his own.

Again, none of these reports were shown to us following Lareau's evaluations that night, so my family and I were basically in the dark as to the seriousness of Lareau's injuries.

GETTING THE DOCTORS' REPORTS

All we could do was wait for one or more of the doctors to give us more information. There seemed to be no change of the prognosis: *There's only a two percent chance that he'll live through the night.*

During that long dark night, I remember giving an aide Lareau's medical information. Fortunately I had the Power of Attorney on record and in Lareau's medical records on file.

I wanted to stay with my husband, but I knew there were other things I had to do. Jeff and I left the ICU – Jeff to update Reese and Jodi, and I called home to notify others. I first shared the news with our daughter-in-law, Jan.

Then I asked Jan to phone one of my best friends, Carol Evans (her husband John was Chairman of Barnabas International's board of directors). I told Jan to give Carol the dire news of Lareau's accident that I'd just shared with her.

We hung up, leaving Jan to call Carol while I called Tom Clinton, a Barnabas staff member, and asked him to start calling the office staff and the other ministry teams.

Chapter Five

Get the Word Out: Pray for Lareau!

Those first two calls by Jan and me around 3:00 a.m. generated the start of several global prayer chains. First Carol Evans called Joe Musser, sharing the terrible news with him: "Please pray for Lareau, the doctors have given him little hope, he might not even be alive by morning."

Joe then phoned his longtime friend Dr. Rochunga (Ro) Pudaite, founder of Bibles for the World, to pray for their mutual friend, Lareau Lindquist.

Dr. Pudaite in turn made a phone call to northeast India, Manipur, where it was the middle of the afternoon. Ro Pudaite reached Rev. Ruolneikhum (Khuma) Pakhuongte. Khuma was the president of the Evangelical Free Church of India (EFCI).

Khuma also knew Lareau and his Barnabas ministry, so he quickly called his staff and pastors to rally Christians from the EFCI churches for a special prayer service for Lareau. The difference in the time zones meant that it was already early evening in northeast India by the time Khuma reached church leaders, who in turn attracted thousands of people who stayed well into the night on "Prayer Mountain" to pray specifically that God would spare their American brother in Christ.

The prayer vigils went all through that horrific night and the next day and continued over several days. I wasn't even aware that prayer vigils had sprung up in India, and later in Kenya, Africa, and spontaneously in many other places around the world.

When Tom Clinton started phoning his list of people, he wanted them to know that Lareau was in the hospital with just a two percent chance of still being alive before daylight, so requesting prayer for Lareau was Tom's most urgent assignment.

Tom first called Perry Bradford, who was Associate Director of Barnabas International. Perry next called Dottie Campbell, the ministry's executive secretary. The three of them manned phones the rest of the night and much of the next day to get the word not only to the dozens of Barnabas staff members but also to Lareau's many friends.

Perry used the Internet to spread the urgency of Lareau's condition by modifying the Barnabas International website, updating it periodically after that terrible first night.

The subsequent chain of phone calls triggered even more prayer partners who then started prayer chains of their own. Another incredible group of hundreds of praying Christians was in the Dondori slums of Nairobi, Kenya, where Lareau had been before his terrible wreck.

Pastor Benson in Nairobi was so touched by Lareau's

predicament that he wanted to fly to the United States and stay in Rockford to be by Lareau's bedside to pray. I told Pastor Benson, "Lareau is still unconscious and the doctors tell us he won't be responsive for some time." I also said that Lareau was plugged into medical machines and new technology to keep him alive. I assured Pastor Benson that instead of flying to America he should bring his people together to pray for Lareau.

Later, I learned that he did bring together 3,000-plus African Christians to pray for Lareau, pleading with God to not let him die. I didn't know about that fantastic event until much later.

I also learned later about many more prayer vigils for Lareau's desperate situation. They sprang up in churches and small groups in America and overseas.

Spontaneous prayer groups gathered in Africa, South America, India, and other locations where Lareau was well known. A number of people who didn't even know him also came together to pray that God would let him live.

Richard Howell, the president of the Evangelical Fellowship of India (EFI), led prayer among many churches. The Evangelical Alliance Churches (TEAC), started by The Evangelical Alliance Mission (TEAM), also held prayer meetings. Romeo Fernando, a Catholic lay leader from Vasai, near Mumbai (Bombay), led prayer vigils with other Catholic lay leaders, sending their deeply emotional, faith-filled pleas heavenward so that God would hear their prayers for Lareau.

There are several other mission organizations like Wycliffe Bible Translators, Greater Europe Mission, The Evangelical Alliance Mission (TEAM), Wycliffe's aviation partner JAARS,

Inc., MAF (Mission Aviation Fellowship), and others whose people also prayed.

Besides the India prayer vigils on the other side of the world, leaders of Willowbank Conference Center in Bermuda also prayed for Lareau when the word came to them as they were just rising. Two time zones between us meant they were already seeing the sunrise as they prayed – a sunrise that the doctor had said Lareau wouldn't live to see.

Other ministries based in the Bahamas had many times brought Lareau and me to their organizations, so when they got the word of his accident, they rallied to pray for Lareau's life.

It was late morning in Europe where Cheryl and Charlie Warner, a Barnabas International staff couple, were living when word reached them. Later that year after Lareau's recovery, his first trip included an inter-mission dinner with some 120 missionaries in Vienna, Austria, which the Warners hosted.

At that event, an American woman, Tammy Neal, related her reaction when she first heard the news of Lareau's accident. She said, "I never met Lareau, but I was a missionary from an international organization based in Illinois. When I heard that the Barnabas founder was near death, I fell to my knees, crying and praying with deep emotion. I prayed to God, 'Lord, don't take this man! He founded an organization to help missionaries and Christian leaders. We need this man! Please keep him alive!'"

Tammy saw the answer to her prayer when Lareau spoke to the missionaries assembled that night.

* * *

GET THE WORD OUT: PRAY FOR LAREAU!

After Lareau was first brought to the emergency room, Tom Clinton left the Barnabas office and drove to the hospital to be with me. After I shared with him what little I knew, Tom began hunting for a Gideon Bible, saying, "I couldn't find one in the waiting room."

"I saw a huge Bible on a stand in the chapel," I told Tom, pointing to where it was. Moments later Tom came from the chapel lugging a huge pulpit Bible, but it served the purpose. Later Tom told me about the various leaders he and Perry had reached to get the word out to pray for Lareau's life, and he wanted to share their Bible encouragements.

At the time I didn't know that any of these remarkable prayer events were already happening across the planet. Jeff and I spent many hours in the hospital waiting room, trusting God's mercy for Lareau. During those long hours, however, there were very few scraps of information available.

Neither Jeff, nor his siblings and I, could accept the doctor's words: *there's only a two percent chance that he'll live through the night.*

Those were the dark moments when I was confronted with the reality that my husband could be dying. I tried to banish those thoughts as quickly as they came, but they still came periodically throughout that frightful first night.

We hadn't been allowed to see Lareau after we got that first glimpse of him in the ICU. The reason was that more than a dozen people were coming into the ICU – physicians, anesthesiologists, surgeons, neurologists, dental and plastic surgeons, ophthalmologists, and nurses – responding to the needs of the man who was expected to die before morning.

After a while, I noticed that there were fewer medical people going into the ICU, so I asked if I could have another few minutes with my husband. A nurse who knew me as one of the night shift nurses nodded her head and showed her sadness by biting her lower lip after I asked.

It was much darker in the ICU than in the waiting room, and my eyes had to adjust to the darkness. I walked slowly over to the bed where Lareau was lying – no real life in his body, except that which the machines created.

A respirator helped him breathe, plasma and saline drips fortified his blood, various pharmaceuticals regulated his heartbeats and respiration, and each was clicked off by small chirps of the monitor.

Lareau was not conscious of any of this – he was in a deep coma. At that moment his future seemed dark, and I had a hard time averting thoughts of his dying.

Is it true? Would Lareau die before the long night ended? Will he die before I have a chance to say good-bye?

Standing near his bed, I felt so vulnerable. Yet I refused to think about life without him. Logically it seemed that the doctors and surgeons were right – that Lareau's injuries were so overwhelming that his battered body and his will might give up.

I refused to accept the idea that Lareau would die. I pleaded with God to spare him. In that darkened ICU, my heart ached for a miracle. I prayed for it to happen, but there were no bright lights and angels beaming down from the skies.

I felt no presence in the room to assure me. Only the hissing, clicking, and muffled chirping of the monitoring equipment. Nothing had changed.

GET THE WORD OUT: PRAY FOR LAREAU!

Lareau was strapped to a gurney because his height was greater than the length of a hospital bed. His head and neck were immobilized by a hard metallic collar to protect him from further harm.

There was a gash over the bridge of his nose – one that ran up over his left eye. That eye wasn't bandaged, and I shuddered to see the bone of his upper cheek and eye socket exposed. His eyes were swollen shut.

Instead of hearing his breathing, I heard the sound of a machine pushing oxygen into his lungs. I had no idea if his lungs were punctured or otherwise compromised.

I watched him lying still, seemingly lifeless except for the quiet chirps of the heart and lung monitors and other machines.

It seemed quite strange to see my husband that way, even though over the years I had dealt with hundreds or even thousands of other patients professionally. This time I felt alone and frightened. Perhaps the ICU setting was smothering me with a feeling of helplessness.

As a nurse I'd seen many people in similar critical situations, and I knew from experience that little things are noted. Those clues often lead the family to expect the finality of life.

One or more critical organs might fail. Breathing, heart failure, brain damage. Any of a number of things can cause a body to stop functioning, and a patient as injured as Lareau might easily slip away.

Several times I had to brace myself, expecting to watch Lareau pass away. It seemed to be inevitable. At times I felt wet tears fall onto my cheeks, and I had to bite my lip to keep from bursting out into uncontrollable sobs.

LESS THAN TWO PERCENT CHANCE

I walked closer, with my hand reaching tenderly to touch the hand of my husband, and I was surprised that his hand was so cold. I put my hand on his to warm it. After a moment of holding his hand, I felt better. There was no reason for it. No signs appeared on the monitoring readouts. Nothing had changed. Yet I felt suddenly calm.

Then unexpectedly, as my hand was holding Lareau's, there was a flutter and then a small squeeze, hardly perceptible. Earlier I felt a flutter, but this was a tiny squeeze in response to this touch, and I gasped out loud.

He's there! He's still inside his body! He's not giving up!

Chapter Six

Facing the Horror

Jeff stayed with me through that frightening night while the doctors tried to help keep my husband alive. There were no promises. Jeff and I knew much about such accident injuries in our hospital professions.

The doctors are generally restrained when family or friends ask for a patient's chances. They nearly always exercise caution toward loved ones, raising neither false hope nor despair.

Doctors and surgeons are often more open regarding information for a colleague who's a family member of the patient in question. A conversation between two medical people yields more information than ordinary people receive. They usually share more readily what the patient's prognosis is when both understand the consequences of the injuries.

Those who work in a hospital or medical environment already know the gist of what's going on. So I asked what their consensus was for Lareau, considering all the injuries that he'd received.

One of the lead surgeons was at first reluctant to respond to the question, but I persisted. "You know Jeff and I already have a logical sense of the worst. We work in hospitals, doing what you're doing, so please don't put us off. Tell us what you think." The doctor paused and then said, "Honestly, Evie, you know the statistics. The ER team and the surgeons think that there's barely a chance that Lareau will make it. I'm sorry."

Jeff and I expected words like those. After spending hours during most of that night in the waiting room, hoping for good news from the doctors, we expected the worst, yet we were afraid to face it. Now the words of the doctor had nearly crumpled my body and brain. It was what I expected to hear but didn't want to. I was hoping for a reprieve for Lareau.

Jeff and I dragged ourselves back to the waiting room – to wait. During the long and lonely hours, we received only scraps of information, like rations being doled out to starving people, and the information seemed to be only bad news.

That dire prospect given by the doctor hours earlier gave us no encouragement that their efforts could offer us a miracle. Yet I was buoyed by that earlier moment in the ICU when I felt Lareau's hand lightly squeeze my hand. It convinced me that he was alive and fighting to stay alive, and I had to hang on to that slim thread of hope.

During those early hours before dawn, the medical team had stabilized Lareau and placed him in an induced coma before bringing him to the ICU floor. (At the time I didn't know about the induced coma, but I thought it was customary.)[2]

The doctors had stopped his bleeding and started his

---

2   Lareau and Evie didn't know until some years later when they received Lareau's copies of the doctors' records of their work.

breathing with a ventilator, replacing the emergency tracheotomy the paramedics had made either in the wrecked car or in the ambulance while rushing him to the hospital.

Nothing was done to Lareau's face and chest, where frightening facial cuts, broken bones, and fractured ribs were waiting for repair. It was too early to try to deal with repairing the bones and plastic surgery. I had a hard time looking at Lareau's still body; I couldn't even recognize my own husband! His head was swollen to twice its size, and his facial features looked grotesque in the dim light.

My heart ached to see him in such trauma. My only comfort was the fact that Lareau was unconscious. If he were not sedated, he would be in agonizing pain.

Fortunately, Jeff and I were not completely afraid of the scary-looking patient and the overwhelming technology keeping him together because we both routinely saw such wounds and equipment during our work. Still, the horrible damage to Lareau's head, face, and chest was difficult for us to see. He was lying so still, so fragile.

I really knew that with God in charge nothing is an accident. The whole thing was overwhelming, but it did not move my faith. Despite inordinate odds, I believed Lareau would live through the night.

A nurse was there to look after him and make sure nothing compromised the induced coma until Lareau's body began to recover. Jeff and I sat on the hard, stiff side chairs in the ICU to watch over Lareau. Those chairs were not made for comfort, yet they comforted me by letting me be near Lareau. At least I knew that, so far, he was still alive.

This ordeal turned out to be the longest night of my life. I'm sure that Jeff felt the same. Not knowing what was happening inside Lareau's body and brain was hard for me to endure.

Doctors Towne (the anesthesiologist) and Sollender (a plastic surgeon) and several other doctors who came to the ICU were making assessments of Lareau's injuries and laying out a plan to do further treatment when he responded to the immediate emergency surgery and other care. I could guess what was happening based on who was at Lareau's side at various times.

Dr. Sollender had treated Lareau's initial injuries in the emergency room, right after the ambulance brought him to the hospital. He immediately began surgery on Lareau's face, wrapped his chest, and later attended to a broken rib. His first concern had been for brain damage or heart failure, but fortunately Lareau's exceptional health had tempered those worries.

We had no idea how long the recovery might take.

Sometime later in the early hours of the approaching day, more doctors came to see Lareau. Despite his facial injuries, they wanted to determine what to do when the patient was able to submit to the additional pain and discomfort from further treatment.

First, an orthopedic doctor explained that he'd take bone grafts, after which a surgeon would then use the grafted bone pieces to remake Lareau's cheek bones, replace his sinus cavities, and rebuild his nose. Finally, a surgeon would rebuild Lareau's jaw when he woke from his coma.

After that an internist told us they would determine what kind of rehab Lareau would need, followed by a different rehab to help Lareau learn to swallow and chew.

FACING THE HORROR

Despite all the planned treatments, the doctors were conservative about their operations and expected "fixes" of Lareau's skull, face, and jaw. They were cautious about the work and said such things as, "There are still serious issues, and we are hoping for the best," and, "Some of the repairs might never be possible." All the medical team assigned to Lareau were busily making plans for assessments to help the patient recover.

My children and I spent most of the coming week in the ICU and then in a hospital room set aside for our use, while Lareau continued to be sedated. Not much changed, as the medical teams moved ahead in scheduling those plans that were being made for my husband's recovery.

The second day after the car crash, Lareau's friend Otis Skillings came to the hospital to visit him, even while Lareau was still unconscious. Nevertheless, Otis showed up.

Otis had accompanied Lareau on trips overseas, providing music to complement Lareau's speaking. Often he had even written songs that came from Lareau's sermons. Otis was a close friend.

Otis seemed to be there every day that Lareau was in the hospital. He prayed for Lareau and often came to sing to him and offer encouragement, even though Lareau was still unconscious.

I felt my husband had some awareness of consciousness, and it seemed to me that Lareau could sense it when Otis came to pray and sing.

In addition to local visitors, Lareau also received numerous cards and letters from people around the world. During his hospital stay, Lareau received phone calls and letters from his friend Dr. Wesley Duewel, President Emeritus of OMS

International and a prolific author. Lareau later received Dr. Duewel's international bestselling book *Touch the World Through Prayer*.[3] After his recovering, Lareau took great encouragement from that book along with its great spiritual insights about the power of prayer.

---

3   *Touch the World Through Prayer*, published by Zondervan, 1986.

Chapter Seven

Evie and a Heroic Angel

The TV news and local *Rockford Register Star* articles about Lareau's automobile crash on Alpine Road shocked many when the word got out of my husband. As some of the stories were shown, I noticed the comments or reports of how a young nurse had saved Lareau's life by doing cardiopulmonary resuscitation (CPR) to keep him breathing and his heart pumping.

I wished then that I knew the name of that nurse, so I could seek her out to thank her for saving my husband's life during the desperate moments before the first responders arrived. At first the woman's identity was not reported, but if she was a nurse, it would be easier to track her down.

A few days after the Alpine Road crash, I got a call from Candace, who was caring for our grandchildren while we were at the hospital. Candace told me she'd a received a call from her friend Rita Versendaal. Rita said she had been with the nurse in the news and in their car when the nurse's husband stopped to check out the crash right after it happened.

Candace asked Rita to call me to reveal the identity of our angel in disguise. Rita called and said that she was with Kristin Dolphin, the nurse whose name was not mentioned in the various news accounts.

Rita said, "Kristin is a cardiology nurse, exactly the kind of help Lareau needed when his heart and breathing stopped." I felt the hair on my neck stand out as Rita pointed that out. It was true. It was as if God had sent an angel with the right talents to help Lareau during the critical moments following the crash.

Rita also said that Kristin kept both his heart and breathing functioning until the first responders and ambulance team showed up. Then Rita gave me Kristin's name and address.

I wanted to phone Kristin but initially couldn't find her number, which turned out to be unlisted. That frustrated me, but our mutual friend, Rita Versendaal, had Kristin's phone number, and she gave it to me.

At last, I could finally call Kristin, the heroic nurse who saved Lareau's life!

Soon after our introductions, I asked if we could get together at the hospital, perhaps before or after her shift at the cardiology facility.

"Yes, Mrs. Lindquist. I'd be pleased to meet with you. I've met you before, and I know you because I always loved hearing your stories about your missionary travels overseas, and we cross paths in the hospital too."

We chatted on the phone for several minutes about both of us being nurses, and we made an appointment to get together.

The meeting with Kristin would become very emotional for both of us.

The next afternoon Kristin came to Lareau's hospital room. Prior to her visit to the hospital, neither of us had direct knowledge of the other about the crash. Until the TV news and the local newspaper identified Lareau as the victim in the Alpine Road crash on Friday night, neither of us had known who the other was.

I immediately recognized Kristin when she walked in. She was a nurse, too, as was reported in the media. I'd seen her before at the hospital, but now, as she stood there by Lareau's bed, I saw her face differently. Her countenance seemed to shift in alternating mixes of sadness, sorrow for his injuries, and joy and wonder that he was still alive.

Maybe Kristin had the same response I had the previous Saturday morning – the time that was supposed to be Lareau's day to die. Graciously, God had a different outcome for my husband.

Lareau was still sedated, but the swelling in his head and chest had started to ease. Kristin went to his bedside and looked intently at the man she had helped last Friday night. "He doesn't look like the man in the crash," she whispered.

I wondered what was going through her mind, standing at the foot of Lareau's bed. "He looks badly beaten," Kristin said. Then she added, "But his face seems serene, as if he's at peace."

"That could be the medications," I replied with a smile. We both giggled. After a moment we walked across the room to sit down in the side chairs to talk. "Tell me what happened last Friday night."

Kristin took off her winter coat and draped it on the back of her chair before sitting down. She looked into my eyes as if wondering how to begin. "His accident's been with me every moment I'm awake – even before I heard on the radio that it was Pastor Lindquist."

"I'm sure," I whispered.

"That's when I saw real meaning in what I was able to do for him last Friday night. I mean, yeah, I'm a nurse. You know what it's like. You face the trauma and do your best, but then the patient or victim gets taken to the next stage for recovery and healing, or he or she dies. Either way, we still go on with our other duties."

I nodded, knowing what she meant. "However, your husband's accident was quite special. I mean, I don't recall I've ever met him in person, and even if I had, his face was so swollen, cut, and bloody. Even if I *had* met him, I couldn't know him in that condition."

She paused as if she was recalling the sight of Lareau's injuries of Friday, so I reached over to comfort her. "Kristin, when they let me into the ICU after his hours in the ER, even I couldn't recognize him."

There was silence for a long moment, then I changed the subject. "Kristin, you told me on the phone that it wasn't until two days after the crash that you learned the man you saved was Rita's former pastor at First Free Church."

Kristin turned her gaze to the hospital bed where Lareau was lying, asleep from an induced coma.

I continued with my thought. "Tell me about Friday evening.

How did it happen that you were there? Every person who saw you there at the scene said *you* saved his life."

"*God* saved his life," she said, shaking her head as if correcting me.

"Yes, He did. But it's likely God set up the special circumstances for you to be at the right place at the right time to help save Lareau's life."

I told her, "Everyone – the fire department's EMT guys, the ambulance drivers, and the people on the scene – they all said if it weren't for you, my husband would have died at the scene."

Kristin looked up, tipping her head toward Lareau's hospital bed. "Still, it was God who did all that. I believe *He* led us to the crash site. There were very complicated things I did that night, with shifting of time and place."

I nodded, and I could understand how God would orchestrate her path that night.

Kristin said, "Even though I know God put me there at the right time, I wasn't the only one who helped. Many others were there too. A couple of guys were shouting encouragement to the person pinned inside the car. They kept yelling, 'Keep breathing! Don't stop breathing,' and things like, 'Hang on, mister. Don't give up!'"

Kristin seemed reluctant to accept the credit she'd earned Friday night, so I changed the subject a bit. "Kristin, how *did* you happen to be at the crash site the other night?"

She thought for a moment and then smiled. "It was a remarkable night. I've thought about it over and over. It's as if God had planned everything we did that night. Yes, we did what we could and didn't do things that we shouldn't. Everything seemed to have its own schedule and agenda, like being in a real stage play."

"How's that?" I asked.

"My husband and I went out for dinner with some friends. We stopped to pick up Rita before going to the restaurant. Brad, one of our friends, was late, so we waited for him before ordering. After a while someone called him on his cell phone. Brad said he was on his way and told us to order for him.

"We did order, but for some reason, the meals took more time than usual, and we were getting a bit impatient about the slow service. Finally, the meals came, and eventually so did Brad. We finished our meals but had to wait for Brad to finish. We were probably there at least an extra hour more than we planned. Finally, we were ready to go home.

"We almost forgot that my husband Jeff was going to drive Rita home. He decided to first drop me off at home to put our little two-year-old boy, Keegan, to bed while he took Rita home. Jeff said, 'Let's take a moment to show Rita the work being done in the bathroom, and you can bring Keegan in and I'll take Rita home.'

"But I said, 'No, I'll wait here for you guys.' It's strange. I don't know why I said that. When Rita and Jeff came back to the car, they wondered why I hadn't taken Keegan inside.

"I had no reply, because I didn't know why I stayed in the car – maybe Keegan was asleep in the back. Anyway, when Rita and Jeff got back into the car, I put my seat belt back on, and we all went to take Rita home."

I nodded but didn't say anything, letting Kristin continue. In a quiet voice she said, "We live on Warren Avenue, and taking Rita home meant we'd take Rural to Alpine Road, just two blocks from where your husband crashed his car. We must have missed the collision by only minutes."

I had been holding my breath as Kristin talked, but now I saw what she was thinking and told her, "If you had been earlier, or later, you wouldn't have been able to help Lareau. God did truly manage your schedule that night. Wow!"

The two of us sat there quietly for a moment or two, and then Kristin said, "At first my husband went to see if someone was injured in the crash, and when he saw the driver wedged under the dash and steering wheel, he waved for me to come because I'm a nurse. Rita stayed in the car with Keegan, and Jeff began directing traffic on Alpine while I went to see if I could help the man in the car.

"Someone else was looking inside the car and yelled to those around him, 'He doesn't seem to be breathing! Does anyone know how to do CPR?' That's when I decided to help."

Kristin smiled as she continued her story. "I had a hesitation when I climbed into the car's passenger seat window. That's when I saw how big he was. Not heavy, but tall. He seemed to be wrapped around the gearshift and under the steering wheel. The only thing that came to my mind was, *How did such a tall man get into such a small car?*"

"I have often had the same question come into my mind too, Kristin. Did you have trouble trying to get to him? And, the people looking inside said Lareau wasn't breathing. Is that right?"

Kristin shook her head. "No, it was just very shallow. I just worked to get him up so I could assess his wounds. I checked his mouth, his nose, and wiped blood from his face so he didn't choke. Then I tried to guess what injuries he'd received. I saw that his head and face caught much of the impact of the steering wheel. I didn't see any broken ribs sticking out of his skin or other serious wounds in his chest and sides of his torso. There could've been invisible wounds, like bruised or injured heart muscles."

I asked, "How could you have taken his vitals, pulse and breathing, and so forth? I mean, the way he was twisted and hard to reach?"

"You know, it all happened intuitively. I've been in hospital emergencies and things like that. But that accident was an incredible timeline that seemed to happen in a remarkable way. I was helping, but I relied upon instinct more than anything."

"You certainly had the right instincts, Kristin. You must have had much experience to be able to pull all your instincts together."

"I think it was God's presence with me in that car," Kristin said softly. "I mean, I'm a cardiology nurse. That's my field. I was a little nervous that I was facing a man with other injuries as well. He might have had a seizure, a stroke or any kind of event that could have forced him off the road."

Kristin looked my way, trying to soften the possibilities. "Or he might have a broken pelvis or a broken spine, maybe even massive damage to the brain from the impact.

"I thought of all those things and sent God a prayer to help me. I'm not sure what was going on in my mind then. All I could do was keep my thoughts on helping the victim."

Then Kristin recalled something. "One of the things that

freaked me out was when I touched his cheek to open his mouth for broken bone fragments or teeth," she said.

"Freaked out?"

"When I touched his face, it was puffy. I pushed on his cheek, and it felt like a bubble wrap 'squish' when I cleared his mouth and removed the nose full of debris to keep him breathing. That was something I'd never before seen in any emergency room situation," Kristin said in her soft voice.

I asked, "When the fire department EMTs and ambulance came, what did they do to help?"

"They were very professional and serious. They checked to make sure that there wasn't any gasoline leaking that could cause an explosion, and the EMT guys tried, but failed, to open both car doors. That's when they decided to use the Jaws of Life to get into the vehicle itself."

"What did that involve?" I asked.

"It's a huge pneumatic tool that cuts through the metal and lets them peel away enough metal to bring out the victim. I pled with them that there wasn't enough time for that. I was doing CPR to keep him going, but time was running out."

Inwardly I shuddered, thinking of all the threats that could've killed Lareau while he was still in the wrecked car. Instead, I simply nodded.

Kristin continued her story. "I told them the victim would die if we took the time to do all that. So one of the firemen decided he'd climb into the car as I'd done. He wiggled into a squatting position behind the front seat to try to get Lareau onto the front seat.

"Then they used a wide board to bring him out the side

window, first onto a stretcher, then onto the ambulance gurney, and drove off to the hospital. That's when I went back to our van where Rita was watching Keegan."

"You must have been relieved that they got Lareau out of the car and into the ambulance, since the hospital was only about two or three miles away," I said.

Kristin sighed deeply and tried to recall that moment. "There were two police cars taking care of traffic, so Jeff was already in the van when I walked back to Rita and my son, Keegan.

"They wanted to know how it turned out. As I tried to remember it all, I told Jeff and Rita some of my thoughts. We also talked about how his car was the only one in the collision. Somehow the car had swerved around or through the traffic on a single path and smack into that tree." Kristin paused, recalling how fortunate that no other vehicles were involved. "Let's give God credit for that, too."

Then she added, "The last words I recall before we left the site was when I was overwhelmed with the sadness and despair of watching the ambulance leave with him. My thought was: *This man isn't going to make it.*"

We both were quiet, and neither spoke for moments. Then we stood and held each other in a grateful embrace.

For Kristin, it was the repudiation of her fearful thoughts at the accident scene – that Lareau would not survive. Now it almost seemed a happy ending.

For me, I was so grateful that God had placed this very modest, capable young woman, my heroic angel, at the right place and exactly the right time to save my husband's life.

EVIE AND A HEROIC ANGEL

* * *

Some time later Kristin received awards from the American Red Cross and the American Heart Association for her heroic efforts in helping save Lareau's life. This media coverage enabled her to tell others about her experiences. She made certain that she credited God's intervention to save Lareau's life at the site of the accident.

I told Kristin about prayers around the world that were reported to us through the Barnabas office. "We weren't even aware of the hundreds, maybe thousands, of prayer meetings and vigils all across the United States and in many other countries around the world.

"We'd heard from individuals and Christian groups who felt a leading of God to pray for Lareau," I told Kristin. "We know – it's God who intervened for Lareau."

Kristin nodded and then said, "I know how true that is. I've heard people say, 'You were lucky to come on the scene of the accident.' Or, 'Lareau was lucky to survive.' But *luck* had nothing to do with it.

"I know how powerful prayer is. Nowadays when I hear about remarkable recoveries, even as serious as Lareau's injuries, I tell people that such miraculous recoveries aren't a matter of luck. I don't use the phrase, 'You were lucky!' anymore. Instead, I now know it was God who intervened."

Chapter Eight

How Can You Replicate Someone's Face?

While my husband was still sedated in the early days after the car crash, the plastic surgeon, Dr. Jonathan Sollender, had asked me to provide him with some recent photos of Lareau to see what he was up against in trying to reconstruct his face. All I could come up with was the printed Barnabas International information card with the two of us that we handed out to our friends.

I had known Dr. Sollender through my work as a nurse at the hospital. I suspected that he knew me well – kidding me often about replacing *my* face, having seen me many times at work. However, to my knowledge, the plastic surgeon had never seen Lareau before the crash.

I started having misgivings. Could a plastic surgeon, who didn't know what Lareau looked like before the accident, create a replica of his face by looking at a two-dimensional image

LESS THAN TWO PERCENT CHANCE

in a 4-by-5-inch photo? It was another fear, among others – a fear for me to confront all alone.

I prayed for Lareau almost around the clock. My anxiety rose as I talked to God about this decision, one of many serious decisions I faced, but this one was different.

How could this surgeon, who was as skilled as his reputation but a complete stranger prior to the accident, how could he know how to fix Lareau's face? Wouldn't he need to know him better?

Some time later, I saw Dr. Jerome Weiskopf, another plastic surgeon who is a family friend, who was doing his own rounds at the hospital when he heard of Lareau's accident.

He learned Lareau was in the ICU after barely surviving the crash. After completing his rounds, Dr. Weiskopf came to visit Lareau and saw me there.

I told him about the crash and how miraculously a nurse had kept Lareau alive at the crash site, before the emergency first responders came onto the scene. I related how the hospital team received Lareau and immediately worked to save his life – some skeptical of success based on the doctor's estimate of a two percent chance that Lareau would not live through the night.

After Dr. Weiskopf and I chatted, I changed the subject to my concerns for Lareau. Since we were friends, I looked at him directly and asked *him* to do Lareau's facial surgery.

"You know what Lareau looked like before the accident," I said. I told him of my concern about having another plastic surgeon work from a tiny photo.

"I believe that you can do the reconstruction because you've known him and have had more contact with Lareau."

HOW CAN YOU REPLICATE SOMEONE'S FACE?

I reminded Dr. Weiskopf that he'd even been on a tour to Russia and Ukraine with Lareau and me. "You've been with Lareau several times. You know him and what his face looked like. Please, do the surgery on Lareau's face."

Dr. Weiskopf knew another other plastic surgeon already planned the surgery for Lareau for Monday or Tuesday following the auto crash Friday night.

He shook his head. "I'm sorry. He's the lead surgeon. He'd be the one who normally does that surgery," he explained. "I don't see how I could . . ."

"Please, doesn't our family have a decision on this matter? We want to have a voice about this," I told him.

Jerry Weiskopf was a real friend of ours, and I wanted him to do the plastic surgery for Lareau's face.

And, since he was our friend, he must have known I was right – that he'd be absolutely the best choice for doing Lareau's facial reconstruction.

He had seen Lareau's face countless times – his smile, his expressions, joyful, serious, and his laughter. Jerry Weiskopf was also the one our family wanted.

I reminded him that the other plastic surgeon, though he was also a capable, brilliant surgeon, had never seen Lareau before the crash, which meant he'd never seen the real Lareau.

Dr. Weiskopf paused and listened to my request. Then he put his arm on my shoulder, and he said quietly, "I'll see what I can do."

* * *

Not long after that, Dr. Weiskopf came again to see Lareau, still sedated in the ICU. Once again I told him I wanted him to be the surgeon to repair Lareau's face, instead of a doctor who'd never met Lareau.

"Well, it makes sense. I do know what Lareau looks like, and I'd be pleased to do the surgery. If you prefer to have me do it, I'm sure that the hospital will okay it."

I was elated for the first time since I came to the hospital after the crash. My request to use Dr. Weiskopf was approved. He'd be the surgeon to do the facial reconstruction on Lareau's face on Monday.

However, that decision would not work out. In a frightful turnabout, Dr. Weiskopf would not be the surgeon for Lareau's facial reconstruction. We didn't know then what happened between the time when Dr. Weiskopf received the approval to be Lareau's surgeon and the time it came to do it.

That switch to use the original surgeon was not personal, nor a clash of egos. Instead, other dramatic events made it unable to happen.

* * *

Dr. Weiskopf had previously planned to fly his personal airplane to Cleveland to spend the weekend with his mother, but he changed the flight plan, shorting his visit to his mother. That Sunday was the tenth anniversary of the death of Jerry Wieskopf's father, so the original plans were to be with his mother until Monday, taking her to lunch on Sunday and staying overnight to spend more time with her.

HOW CAN YOU REPLICATE SOMEONE'S FACE?

His previous flight plan had been drawn up well before Lareau's surgery had been scheduled. Dr. Weiskopf told me he'd changed his flight plan to get back late Sunday night, a day earlier than the original stay. The extra time was needed for him to be on the schedule for Lareau's Monday surgery.

Jerry Weiskopf had decided to take off in his single-engine Piper airplane from the Poplar Grove Airport just east of Rockford and fly to Cuyahoga County Airport to visit his eighty-five-year-old mother for a few days in Cleveland, Ohio.

He didn't want to miss such an important date for his mother. It wasn't something from which he'd ordinarily excuse himself, but he explained to his mother that this time he couldn't stay over another day, because he was scheduled for surgery for his close friend, Lareau Lindquist.

So Dr. Weiskopf flew to Cleveland to be with his mother, staying only until evening. Then he went back to the airport and checked out the weather before taking off about 9:00 p.m., Sunday, planning to get back to Rockford later that night. He expected the flight would take only ninety minutes, since there were no serious weather concerns for his return flight. He was an experienced pilot, flying a new plane with advanced electronic aeronautics.

He felt reassured that the trip would be routine and without problems. He took off from Cuyahoga County Airport, contacting the FAA towers along the way to keep abreast of any weather changes.

Toward the end of the hour-and-a-half flight from Ohio to Illinois, Dr. Weiskopf was approaching the Poplar Grove

Airport, east of Rockford. He had a leased hangar there for his new aircraft.

However, at this time of night the Poplar Grove Airport was not manned. When he took off from Cleveland's Cuyahoga County Airport, he had no concern for his landing at the Poplar Grove airstrip. The weather was on his side.

However, while nearing the Poplar Grove landing strip site and shortly after he crossed the Indiana-Illinois line, his plane encountered icy conditions.

Checking the northern Illinois weather, he also noticed turbulence and more icing of the plane over the last half hour. At first, his instruments had told him that the ice wasn't thick enough to cause trouble. But now it was different. He decided not to land his plane at Poplar Grove and instead headed to nearby Greater Rockford Airport, which had longer and wider concrete landing. The Rockford Airport had radar and computer tracking, along with manned control towers and two-way radio communication.

A thick fog and heavy snow began to cloud the sky as Dr. Weiskopf radioed ahead to the Rockford airport tower for permission to land. The tower responded with the current wind speed, directions, and visibility range.[4]

"I've got some turbulence and icing," Dr. Weiskopf radioed to the control tower controller, who then gave him permission to land.

On approach to Rockford Airport, Dr. Weiskopf relied even more on his instrument panel as a mix of snow and rain, icy clouds and darkness virtually obscured the runway.

---

4   These details were reported in a local newspaper, *"Injured Pilot Local Surgeon"* in the *Rockford Register Star,* January 25, 1999.

The tower controller radioed, "Piper Six, you're coming in too high. Do a '360 circle' and approach the runway at lower altitude."

Dr. Weiskopf followed the tower controller's instructions and descended to 1,000 feet, where he could finally see the runway lights. That 1,000-foot altitude ordinarily seems high, unless you're in an airplane. Then it seems very close to the ground. In context 1,000 feet is about the same as a hundred stories of a building, like the height of Chicago's Sears Tower with its 106 stories.[5]

Dr. Weiskopf did his best to keep his airplane turning into the full circle as the Rockford tower told him, and then he began his final approach to land. But when he tried to turn and straighten the airplane's direction, he saw his plane was also seriously losing height because of more accumulating ice, which by now covered the entire airplane. Dr. Weiskopf realized his landing was suddenly terribly compromised. *I'm coming in too low!*

Too low meant that he had to get more lift, because his plane was still a half-mile from the runway and dropping faster than he could reach the runway. Jerry Weiskopf was fearful the plane would likely drop too soon, too low, and into snow-covered ground – and not onto the runway.

He tried desperately to get his plane back up to a safer altitude to get that last half-mile to the runway. Looking at the ground blurring past him, he peered through thick icy clouds. He saw

---

5 When the accident took place in 1999, the name of the building was the Sears Tower (1973-2003). Sears Tower was changed in 2003 to Willis Tower when the building was sold.

at the last second that his plane was heading straight toward a high airport security fence.

Dr. Weiskopf told a news reporter later, "That's when I knew I couldn't recover and get lift; the plane had too much ice on the fuselage and wings. I couldn't do anything that'd lift the plane high enough, quickly enough, and still maintain airspeed. It was a sinking feeling when I lost power."

There was no time left for him to be afraid of what was coming next. It all happened at once.

Piper Six landed almost a half mile from the runway. Losing altitude, it bounced onto the frozen field with its drifted snow; then it plowed through the security fence, which caught a wing just as the plane plowed through. It clipped the wing as easily as a toy.

Dr. Weiskopf recalled later, "I don't remember much about the moment of impact. I recall looking over and seeing the broken wing and someone (a fire department rescue worker) pulling me from the wreckage. And then, the only other memory I have was of being in the ambulance."

It had taken just minutes for the Airport Fire Department to respond to the call for a crash landing. Those first responders rescued Dr. Weiskopf and carried him to the ambulance, then sped him to the intensive care unit at the St. Anthony Medical Center – the same hospital ICU where Lareau was.

Ironically, after bringing Dr. Weiskopf to the hospital emergency room, a medical team stabilized him and put him in the bed next to Lareau's.

Dr. Weiskopf was brought in with a serious condition. He was treated for rib injuries, bruised heart muscle, and a broken

HOW CAN YOU REPLICATE SOMEONE'S FACE?

back. Instead of operating on Lareau Monday, Dr. Weiskopf himself was taken to surgery to repair a crushed vertebra and other less serious injuries.

The hospitalized pilot and plastic surgeon was sidelined from doing Lareau's facial reconstruction operation as we had planned. Instead, Dr. Sollender operated. In answer to many prayers, he did a remarkable job.

Even Dr. Weiskopf had to admire the work of Dr. Sollender. "I thought, for a person who didn't know what Lareau looked like before and operating only based on a photograph, Dr. Sollender did quite a feat."

Chapter Nine

Evie's Encouragement

Days after Lareau's terrible automobile crash the night of January 22, 1999, doctors told me that my husband was making progress, but to me that progress seemed small and slow.

I was getting used to hearing the doctors give me a daily briefing, but to me, while it was progress, Lareau was moving forward ever so slowly, inch by inch. Despite tiny encouragements, there were setbacks as well. Nevertheless, I found comfort and encouragement from Paul's letter to the Christians at Corinth:

> *Thank God, the Father of our Lord Jesus Christ, that he is our Father and the source of all mercy and comfort. For he gives us comfort in our trials so that we in turn may be able to give the same sort of strong sympathy to others in theirs.* (2 Corinthians 1:3-4)

Ironically, I found myself looking for positive outcomes of Lareau's progress. I discovered that each small comfort encouraged me, and when I shared the news, it encouraged my family and friends. That reminded me of another of Paul's comments:

> *We wish you could see how all this is working out for your benefit, and how the more grace God gives, the more thanksgiving will redound to his glory. This is the reason why we never collapse.*
> (2 Corinthians 4:15-16)

I spent my waking hours at the hospital. My family and friends came to our aid, taking care of other matters while I concentrated on my husband's medical issues.

Perry Bradford and Tom Clinton had taken the ball and were keeping the operations of Barnabas International moving along. Yet they were reluctant when it came to a specific task that was only handled by Lareau. It was the monthly newsletter *Encouragement* that he created and by 1999 had published for some thirteen years. Lareau liked to keep the *Encouragement* issues fresh, and he had a knack of finding ideas and anecdotes that lifted the spirits of our several thousand subscribers every month.

Perry called me at the hospital to remind me of the deadline for the next issue. He asked me to write the February newsletter for Lareau and explain what had taken place in the past week or so.

I had to think seriously about that idea, hoping that Lareau would wake up soon and dictate the February issue. With all the daily briefings by the doctors, I wasn't sure that I could make it happen, perhaps in March.

We had already sent information in our prayer appeals

explaining Lareau's near-death experience, so I wasn't sure we needed a February issue. Yet, they asked me to write it.

I prayed about doing that. I saw the value of sharing the news about his condition and the need for prayers for Lareau, so I wrote the February *Encouragement* newsletter, and Perry and office staff printed and mailed it.

Many of our friends and contributors wrote back and assured us of their prayers. Other cards and letters spoke to their own fearfulness, not all problems were as serious as Lareau's injuries, but I was told that our subscribers who wrote to our office said they benefited by my comments.

I decided to use Philippians 4, one of the apostle Paul's greatest messages of comfort. My goal was to find something that could lift the spirits of our friends who read our newsletter. Here's what I wrote:

Encouragement February 1999[6]

Good Morning Friend,

The ventilator is hissing; the monitor above flashes numbers and all sorts of wavy and jagged lines. In front of me lies my beloved husband of thirty-seven years, Lareau.

He's alert, but his condition is critical, and he is unable to speak and frustrated in his "prison" of tubes and wires.

So, where was God when all this happened? Well, He was where He has always been and will be – on His Throne.

He is guiding every moment of our lives into the tapestry He has designed for our lives.

Yes, I am sorrowful – yet rejoicing. Really! Right now I

---

[6] Published by *Barnabas International* Vol. XIII, No. 2.

am thinking of the thousands of you around the world who receive this letter. Some of you are also going through personal and maybe even private tragedies. Others of you are discouraged, questioning God's purpose. I am too. So let's trust His wisdom.

I have just been reading a paraphrase from Philippians 4, given to me by a dear friend:

Don't fret or worry. Instead of worrying, pray. Let petitions and praises shape your worries into prayers, letting God know your concerns. Before you know it, a sense of God's wholeness, everything coming together for good, will come and settle you down. It's wonderful what happens when Christ displaces worry at the center of your life.... I'm glad in God, far happier than you would ever guess – happy that you're again showing such strong concern for me. Not that you ever quit praying and thinking about me. You just had no chance to show it. Actually, I don't have a sense of needing anything personally. I've learned by now to be quite content whatever my circumstances. I'm just as happy with little as with much, with much as with little. I've found the recipe for being happy whether full or hungry, hands full or hands empty. Whatever I have, wherever I am, I can make it through anything in the One who makes me who I am. (Philippians 4:6-7; 10-14 MSG)

This is my testimony, and I pray it's yours too!

Be Encouraged!

Evie Lindquist

I didn't think when March 1999 was upon us that Lareau would still be hospitalized, but he was. I was asked to write another *Encouragement* for March.

Interestingly, I found that when I looked for my own encouragement, I took the task more readily. I found two passages in 2 Corinthians that lifted my spirits:

> *What a wonderful God we have – he is the Father of our Lord Jesus Christ, the source of every mercy, and the one who so wonderfully comforts and strengthens us in our hardships and trials. And why does he do this? So that when others are troubled, needing our sympathy and encouragement, we can pass on to them this same help and comfort God has given us.*
> (2 Corinthians 1:3-4 TLB)

And, this verse:

> *That is why we never give up. Though our bodies are dying, our inner strength in the Lord is growing every day....The troubles will soon be over, but the joys to come will last forever.*
> (2 Corinthians 4:16, 18 TLB)

Those words by the apostle Paul encouraged me, as if he was telling me that we all go through trials to equip our brothers and sisters in Christ.

I used those verses to help my own spirit and have used them often to buoy my spirit but also to encourage others and write a second *Encouragement* newsletter.

Here is a copy of that March letter:

***Encouragement* March 1999**

Good Morning Friend,

Cards of all kinds have come to us – about 350 at last count. All convey kind messages of love, concern, and prayers. One particular card was addressed to me personally. On the front was a sketch of a sheep dangling in midair. The caption said, "The last thing you need is one more person telling you to 'hang in there.'"

Opening the card, it reads, "So I'll just ask God to remind you how secure HIS hold is!" And the inside panels showed two large, sturdy hands holding the front feet of the sheep, now gleefully kicking up his heels with no fear of falling. The tagline said, "HE will never let you down."

I read Psalm 18:16: *He reached down from on high and took hold of me. He drew me out of deep waters* (NIV).

The waters have been deep. Many days I've felt so weak physically, emotionally, and spiritually that I've said, "Lord, please hang on to me; I don't have any more strength." And from the loving hand of the Lord holding on to me, I know that Lareau has sensed this as well.

On my many drives to the hospital, I've heard some of Chuck Swindoll's radio programs on the local Christian station. What struck me most was

God's message: *You can trust Me – for the insurmountable opportunity you've been given.*

An opportunity? Maybe so!

As I've been involved in the hospital vigil, consisting of minutes that become hours. Hours that turn to days, and days to weeks.

Has it been mundane? No! As I've looked back on these past weeks, I have seen opportunities – scores of them. It's sharing with friends and colleagues the reality of God's marvelous power and intervention in our lives, such as giving Lareau's book, *Too Soon to Quit*. I've handed the book to hospital personnel from many departments.

Then, I've been blessed from their feedback. They tell me that reading Lareau's book had also given them encouragement:

Troubles and trials are an opportunity – sometimes such opportunities seem to be insurmountable. But not to our Omnipotent Father. God is a Father who is loving, faithful, and gentle. He always holds us tight with strong hands – even when we're too weak to "hang in there."

This is my testimony. I pray it'll become yours too!

Be Encouraged,

Evie Lindquist

Chapter Ten

Lareau Awakens

Evie told me that I awakened several times during my hospitalization, but I can't remember exactly the time I fully awakened from my induced coma, which had enabled me to heal from the injuries I sustained from the January auto crash that brought me to the hospital.

Doctors had told Evie that there was only a two percent chance that I'd live through the first night of my hospitalization. But God had a different prognosis.

While I was in and out of consciousness at the beginning, I began to understand why I didn't die that night. I believe it was based on great and remarkable prayers that came from far-flung places across the world.

When I regained consciousness, I learned that there were all-night prayer vigils in India, Africa, South and Central America, and meetings across the United States where people gathered. Many didn't even know me but knew one of our friends, coworkers, fellow pastors, or even people who heard about my accident on national Christian radio station news reports.

It would be impossible to know how many thousands were praying for me with prayer vigils in Kenya, Africa, and northeast India in the states of Meghalaya and Manipur. There were at least 3,000 at all-night prayer vigils for me in three separate places alone. Our offices received letters, emails, and phone calls from hundreds, thousands, or more.

I'm totally convinced that I wouldn't have survived that first night without those prayers. As they contacted our Barnabas office, they reported how the prayer meetings began to catch fire, even as the doctors in the emergency room and the operating rooms were frantically trying to save my life.

It was only later that we learned how effective those prayers were. They were a mix of spontaneity and sincerity, heavy with faith that God was listening to their prayers and trusting His love and ability to heal.

All this happened at once in various locations around the world when those prayers went directly to God's ear and immediately miracles took place.

Of course, Evie and I didn't know about these powerful prayers at the time, but we were later overwhelmed by love as stories came in to our office. Most were offering their concern and pleadings – mostly from Christians who didn't even know me. That in itself was incredible, and it took a while for it to sink in to my brain.

We didn't try to accomplish the great prayer avalanche, but we realized it could only be explained as a miracle. Was it a coincidence that I survived? I don't think so.

As mentioned earlier, a doctor had told Evie that there was only a two percent chance that I'd live through the first night. That doctor was not being flippant. He was an intelligent medical specialist, so he knew from experience that his expectation was credible.

I believe God responded to the faith and pleas of His people. When Evie and I got more information, we saw how specific prayer vigils brought corresponding results in the operating rooms, which fostered incredible surgical successes, despite the initial prognosis of the doctors.

God powerfully overruled those who projected "a two percent chance" of my surviving the first night in the hospital.

We believe it was totally because of the hundreds in America and thousands overseas in India and Africa who prayed for my life.

However, for those first days and nights, I was still in a coma, coming in and out occasionally. I can't even recall the exact time I was coherent enough to understand what had happened to me, but as Evie spent most of her time with me, I began to absorb more.

At the same time, painkillers and induced sleep also gave me weird memories. No doubt they were hallucinations or dreams, but I had some strange "memories" from those early days and nights. They seemed to be as real as any experience that one would recall.

Later I figured out that there were two different "conversations" going on. I was under the influence of the medications they gave me. I was in La-La Land (having hallucinations), but I felt coherent enough to talk with Evie or one of my children.

Somehow I blended those two components. First, I had a "memory" of walking through the hospital hall with Evie or one of my kids, and I was confused because I couldn't find the patient we came to visit.

While this "dream-hallucination" was embedded in my brain, I was also lying in a hospital bed when one of my family members or a friend came by to visit me, and my brain had trouble differentiating between what was real and what wasn't.

Of course, there were also times that the medications and painkillers to subdue the pain made me woozy. Yet for the most part, things began to come together, as piece-by-piece, people helped me put the puzzle together.

So as I began to come around to a reasonable reality and get a little more strength, I also took notice of my pain – the pain of my broken bones and my healing surgery sites, as well as my jaw that was wired shut. Despite the pain, I somehow managed to have a fairly optimistic attitude.

Early in my hospitalization, I was really "out of it." The induced coma had its purpose, which was to keep me from bearing the incredible pain from my injuries.

It was probably best that I was unconscious day after day for several weeks. I don't recall when they did repairs on my facial bones, but following that otherwise grueling enterprise, there was residual pain and soreness that lasted for weeks.

The same was true for the initial plastic surgery, done to reconstruct my entire face, which had been destroyed and needed to be rebuilt. Our doctor did some follow-up work. I *do* remember his coming into my hospital room close to midnight one time to take metal staples out of my head. Wow, was that painful!

Although the doctors worked hard to make me look as close to my "real" face as possible, there were still scars to deal with. They did their best surgical artistry to keep my scarring to a minimum.

However, I had a scar on the front of my throat where I had a tracheotomy. Less visible were the scars on my rib cage and the scars covered by my hair.

When I was recovering, Evie gave me a gold neck chain. It was a "welcome back" gift to celebrate my transition from critical condition to stable.

I received another gift from friends who owned a shop in the Bahamas, so I asked him to make me a rough but sturdy cross for Evie's gift chain. He did – a cross which beautifully matched Evie's gold chain.

My friends exceeded my expectations by creating a one-of-a-kind cross. When I first put it on, I noticed that the cross covered the scar of my tracheotomy.

I showed it to Evie and repeated the thought, "The cross covers the scar," and at once we saw a great spiritual truth in that moment – *the Cross covers the scar,* or more to the point, *HIS Cross covers ALL MY scars.*

The two gifts, the chain and the cross, constantly remind me of my crash. They remind me of the ongoing reality of the cross of Christ. Apostle John, in his first epistle, says, *The blood of Jesus, His Son, purifies us of all sin* (1 John 1:7 NIV).

Yet it's not a once-and-for-all event. The apostle John implies by his explanation of Christ's blood on the cross that it keeps on cleansing. It keeps on purifying us.

An older hymn, *Calvary Covers It All*, says essentially the same thing: "Calvary covers it all, my past with its sin and stain; my guilt and despair Jesus took on Him there, and Calvary covers it all."[7]

That's right. Calvary covers it all. Really? Some people think they have some ugly sin in their past. You know, that habitual sin he or she can't seem to shake or the secret sins that no one else knows about. Well, the Bible and these songwriters have it pegged. God's forgiveness covers it all.

I recall someone said: "There are two things about sin that we need to take more seriously from 1 John 1:9. [First] we need to take more seriously our confession of sin. Second, we need to truly believe we are forgiven."

When I wear that gold chain and cross, I recall that Satan, our accuser, will continue to try to tempt us. However, God, our Forgiver, truly cleanses and forgives us. Again, *His Cross covers my scars.*

---

[7] Words and Music by Mrs. Walter G. Taylor, ©1934, renewed 1962, The Rodeheaver Co.

Chapter Eleven

Lareau's Dark Nights – Will God Retire Me?

Many times during my long hospitalization and rehabilitation, it seemed to me that I would never get better, never be capable enough to get back to the only work I've known, the ministry.

Early in the hospitalization, it seemed to me that most of the doctors were concerned only with my survival but not necessarily with my recovery.

At my age (sixty-two years old), they cautioned me that bouncing back from an injury like mine wouldn't be as quick or easy as it would be for a much younger patient. One of those doctors said, "Because of your age, there are a number of anomalies that could keep you from being the man you were before that January car crash. Your age is an obstacle, Lareau."

He wasn't saying that as a final decision. Yet his words sunk into my mind and led me to consider the serious possibility that

I wouldn't be able to fully recover or ever be able to resume my work and ministry with Barnabas International.

It was then that I realized the serious nature of my injuries. The doctors did not encourage much optimism regarding making a full recovery.

Though I tried to be positive, I saw that I was now a person with great deficits. I couldn't will myself to recuperate, not even enough to resume my role as an active minister to missionaries.

If this situation was permanent, what could I really look forward to? Looking ahead was not as clear as looking back. My mind went back to the beginnings of the Barnabas ministry.

* * *

I had a flashback to how Evie and I began the ministry of Barnabas International, the ministry we had established after retiring from my role as senior pastor for First Evangelical Free Church in Rockford, Illinois. I had a series of ministry opportunities, and on one trip we found ourselves unexpectedly detained in a remote jungle area where Wycliffe had a missionary base. It was an experience neither of us would forget.

One night we took a long walk and visited a grave memorial for a martyred missionary, Chet Bitterman, a linguist for the Summer Institute of Linguistics (SIL). When Bitterman went to Colombia, he was not yet an experienced linguist, so he wasn't assigned as a missionary right away. He began to translate the Bible into a new language as most Wycliffe missionaries do. After a while, he was given an area to reach as part of the Wycliffe linguistics mission work.

But on January 19, 1981, seven M-19 guerrillas barged into the group house in Bogota and captured Bitterman, who became a hostage under the control of the terrorists. The M-19 guerrillas' demands included having all SIL linguists leave Colombia. However, forty-eight days after his kidnapping, Chet Bitterman's body was found just outside Bogotá, having been shot in the chest, killed by his captors.

As we read the inscriptions on his grave marker, we noticed that he was born in 1953 and died in 1981; he lived only twenty-eight years. Evie and I remarked on how young Chet Bitterman was when he died, and we realized that there were many more martyrs like Chet Bitterman.

We thought of the enormous numbers of those who died in Burma, India, Korea, Iran, Iraq, in Uganda under Idi Amin, and Pol Pot in Cambodia. There were so many Christians martyred in the latter half of the twentieth century that it was overwhelming compared with martyrs dying for Christ in centuries past.

That evening in a place called Coña Colorado, late into the night, Evie and I found ourselves again walking on the Wycliffe airstrip. I remember how we noticed that the small airstrip and its missionary pilots had become a feature that had helped to expand and develop the overall ministry of that region.

* * *

We also spent another long time at the grave of Chet Bitterman. We discussed how he'd sacrificed his life for Jesus Christ. We talked about whether or not *we* might one day have to give our lives for God's service.

That night we prayed by the memorial site and asked God to use us for missions and ministry. I recall that we even gave over to God the prerogative of giving our lives for Him in our ministry.

But what ministry?

We had been serving God all our lives. Yet our plans were not crystallized, and we had no specific direction. We were eager to have God lead us to a new ministry that would serve His purposes and will and enable us to work together to help others.

Our prayers were lengthy that night, and we sought direction from God asking for a ministry that would use our experience and expertise. We reviewed how we had been invited to help encourage other missionaries overseas in far-flung places where it's difficult for missionaries to find counsel.

It seemed to both Evie and me that God had helped us focus on those missionary ministries, but in addition, He seemed to be leading us to a wider and more in-depth kind of mission.

We thought of the events that brought us to that remote jungle area. Even there we saw the possibility of a wider ministry, perhaps all over the world, where airstrips have really been used of the Lord to facilitate the progress of the gospel.

Now, with an airstrip, missionaries could access another city or even a tribal area that has its own airstrip. It meant that the gospel would grow exponentially because of the airplane.

As we thought of that example, we asked God to give us some kind of exponential growth in our ministry. After much prayer and months of crystallizing our ideas, we had a plan. During those months the concept of Barnabas International became a reality.

We could see innovations like airstrips enlarging a ministry to wider geography and expanding their efforts into greater opportunities. The same thing was taking place in other areas of modernity, including the fledgling computer technology and the similar explosion of satellite radio and television.

Evie and I were familiar with these expanding opportunities, and we often prayed for God's guidance to lead us into a ministry that could expand and develop those mission opportunities in reaching other people with the gospel of Christ.

Our ideas for a ministry needed a name as when we began in 1986. We considered the name "Barnabas" because it has a significant meaning in the New Testament. So the new ministry's name became Barnabas International.

The King James Version of the Bible says that Barnabas means "son of encouragement." There are other interpretations of the name Barnabas, but all seem to derive similar meanings. The book of Acts mentions a Christian convert, *Joseph, a Levite from Cyprus, whom the apostles called Barnabas (which means Son of Encouragement)* . . . (Acts 4:36 NIV).

There were many leaders in the early Christian church, but few were as humble and yet able to be what some organizations call a project manager. Among the early apostles, perhaps none were any more influential than Joseph, nicknamed Barnabas.

Thousands of Jews were converted on the day of Pentecost in Jerusalem and in the days that followed. They stayed in the city to hear the preaching of Peter and the apostles. One of them was Barnabas from Cyprus.

Peter, who had been given the "keys" to the kingdom, was

the one who first preached to the Gentiles. However, God chose Paul to be his anointed preacher to the Gentile nation.

As a new convert, Paul went to Jerusalem and tried to make contact with the believers there, but for the most part they feared him. After all, wasn't he the Jewish religious leader who stood by when a crowd stoned Stephen? And didn't Paul do his best to eradicate this new revolutionary effort of the early Christians?

But after meeting Joseph the Levite, the apostle Paul prepared to go on his early missionary journeys. Joseph was recruited to accompany Paul or go some place on Paul's behalf, and his nickname became Barnabas, "son of encouragement." Barnabas became an encourager to the local church, and he was sent to Jerusalem to encourage those working for the cause of Christ there.

So when Evie and I went to that two-week assignment with Wycliffe Bible Translators in Colombia, South America, in the spring of 1986, the name Barnabas, "son of encouragement," took on a significance for us.

Later that year, when we conceived the ministry of Barnabas International and formed an organization, we felt the spirit of God working in our lives. He helped us pull together a supportive group of Christian leadership as a board of directors for Barnabas, and then we launched it not long afterward.

We started it as a "Ma and Pa" enterprise with no intention of expanding beyond just ourselves. Our strategy was to target missionaries, national church leaders overseas, Christian workers in the United States, and Christians who need encouragement anywhere in the world.

Once we began Barnabas, we saw God bless our efforts, and

He allowed our ministry to expand. Other couples came to join with us in Barnabas to reach out to even more who needed a touch of encouragement in their own ministries.

* * *

Thirteen years had passed with an expanding ministry for Barnabas International. But now, lying in a hospital bed, I needed encouragement myself. I noticed that Evie had also wondered if we could continue in the role we held in those past thirteen years of ministry.

I suspected that Evie's thoughts were something like mine: *Is God telling us that our time of ministry is done? Are we supposed to quit, to retire?*

Well, it was true that I'd be approaching age sixty-five, when many people retire. I was also aware of my limitations and lingering injuries while in the hospital. My injuries seemed even more dire than I'd previously considered. *Maybe I'm supposed to call it quits and retire.*

With the horrific car crash, my injuries, and physical setbacks, I had those thoughts on my mind continually, as I began to come back to reality. It was then that I had lingering concerns about Barnabas and our future.

The daily routine led me to disappointment and anxiety. I began to question God: *Why, Lord? Why me?* Yet, my other "whys," "wheres," "whens," and my doubts made me consider. They were serious thoughts for me.

- *Why didn't God let me die in the crash?*

- *When, if ever, can I get back physically to the way I was before the accident?*
- *Will I ever get my intellect, my physical strength, and other abilities back?*
- *When or will I be able to serve God in ministry? Or, will He retire me?*

There were many more dark nights that were filled with those and similar questions. I had to deal with those doubts and fears.

I was experiencing the blessing of the ultimate boomerang: *For the past thirteen years with Barnabas International, I had a ministry of encouragement to Christians all over the world, but now many others were coming to encourage **me**!*

Chapter Twelve

My Mind and Body in Limbo

My jaw was wired shut, and my body was covered with monitor wires, clamps, and other connections to a ventilator, pulse reader, respirator, heart monitor, catheter, IV drip, a pole with a nutrient drip, and countless other devices and utilities. Of course, these features were there from the beginning, but during my induced coma, I was oblivious to them.

However, one day when I was awake, the medical team put in a feeding tube directly through my abdomen. Much later, after it was removed, my little grandchild came to visit and, of course, noticed the scar there. He said, "Poppa, why do you have two belly buttons?"

I laughed despite some fractured ribs, and it caused me to think of the last time I laughed. I couldn't remember, but it must have been a long time ago.

Eventually I was weaned of my induced coma, and when I had a few episodes of consciousness, Evie always seemed to be in the room with me. Her presence was reassuring to me. I was still heavily sedated with pain-killing drugs, which helped keep the pain in check to some level, but they also had side effects. As I stated earlier, one of those effects was hallucinations. My reality and dreams seemed to overlap.

One time I sensed what seemed real but later was told it was a dream or hallucination. I recalled walking down the corridor of the hospital, looking into the different rooms. I saw patients and thought *I* was there to visit someone, as when I was a pastor making a pastoral visit, when I'd talk and minister to the patient.

However, that scenario was impossible. I couldn't have walked the hospital corridors and talked to other patients. I was strapped down in bed in the ICU, my jaw was wired shut, and bandages surrounded my head, carefully holding the broken bones of my skull to help the bones to heal. In that condition I couldn't possibly talk to anyone; it had to be a hallucination or a dream.

To communicate with each other, Evie helped me write notes of questions and comments. From that she could respond and explain to me what was going on and let me know if I was hallucinating or not.

Over time I eventually learned to discern between reality and drug effects. It was during one of these almost lucid times that Evie told me about the doctor who said the consensus of the ER team that treated me that Friday evening was that I wouldn't live through that fateful night. She said that a doctor told her earlier, *There's only a two percent chance that he'll live through the night.*

But here I was – alive, yet not fully convinced that my life would *continue*. And even though I stayed alive, there was no assurance that I'd be able to function as well as before.

Evie's faith was stronger than mine during that crucial time. I was glad that whenever I was conscious she was there; she stuck with me during the terrible battle to stay alive.

Because of my dark bout with the pain-killing drugs, my mind was often clouded or compromised by the nightmares and hallucinations. It was Evie who was constantly with me, being *my* source of encouragement. She was *my* Barnabas – or rather *Batnabas* (the biblical feminine name for Barnabas).

Evie told me how she knew I was alive when I was in a coma. While doctors despaired about my chances, she sensed a tiny twitch of my hand in hers, and that was all it took to convince Evie that I was still alive inside my traumatized body.

When I "talked" to her from my bed (when my jaw was wired shut) with a notepad, I sometimes shared my concerns about my future – mainly our ministry. I had many questions with no answers. Yet Evie was certain that God had His own plans and that we should wait for Him to reveal them.

"We've had a wonderful thirteen years serving Barnabas," she reminded me. Then she recalled the time in 1986 when we stayed up that July midnight in Coña Colorado near Colombia, South America.

"Remember?" she asked.

I spoke through my notepad: "Of course. We started as a 'Ma and Pa' ministry with no intention of being more than that, but it was the Lord who has blessed and allowed this remarkable ministry of Barnabas to grow and expand."

"That's why I'm sure God will bring you through this,"

Evie said, then added, "However, it might be quite some time, assuming you can be able to get back to what we've been doing the past thirteen years. Let's not get ahead of God."

I winced at her words, and I scribbled on my notepad, "He might arrange for us to step down!"

When she read my few words, I expected that she might think them harsh. Instead Evie took them with compassion and love; still, I felt a heaviness in me.

Evie noticed and tried to put me at ease. She added, "Even if God has other plans for us, and yes, He *might* arrange for us to step down, but *if* He *does,* I'm sure He'll have other plans for us."

I didn't want to hear that. I wondered, *If our ministry is to be taken away, why didn't God allow me die in the crash?* However, I didn't write that somber thought on my notepad.

I'm sure I was feeling psychological pain as well as physical injuries. I didn't want to be overcome by pity or negative feelings, so I was encouraged by my family as well as friends who came to visit me.

Yet here in the hospital, getting information about myself and my future was not always possible, and the longer I was lying in my hospital room, the longer and more frequently I aired my concerns to God.

It even seemed to me that in those dark nights and dreary days, I sensed God refreshing my memories of our recent past. The Lord reminded me of our work, but also the growth of Barnabas. I was reminded how God called many other people to join Barnabas, working with Evie and me in a ministry of encouragement.

As the years passed, dozens of other ministers and missionaries found the Barnabas organization and came aboard, their eager and ready hearts focused on the overall ministry of encouragement.

However, there in the hospital, even Evie wondered, *If we aren't able to continue with Barnabas, what could our roles in ministry be?*

We faced a dramatic quandary – we were nearing retirement age, and with the horrific car crash, my subsequent injuries, and physical setbacks, I had lingering concerns about what would happen next for the ministry that Evie and I had begun. Yet the greater question in my mind was *Why?*

And another question again filled the hospital room: *Why didn't God let me die in the crash?* It wasn't because I was eager to die. To the contrary.

From time to time, I wondered, *Could I ever overcome that terrible night? Can I get back what was lost?*

I was also dogged by three other concerns:

1. Would I have some physical deficits?

2. Would I be able to continue my ministry with Barnabas?

3. Would there be complications that could shorten my lifespan?

"Will I ever be able to serve God again?" That's a question I asked some of my close confidants over the next weeks. They usually tried to be upbeat, but I was still troubled by that question. Looking back, though, I think it was because of those many dark nights with drugs and side effects that often overwhelmed me with negative thoughts. It was at those times that I prayed for the Holy Spirit to give me courage and to help me reject the thoughts Satan was directing toward me.

However, during those dark times I was receiving daily visits from friends and fellow pastors. I've already mentioned how Otis Skillings came to see me almost every morning. He conversed with me, or tried to, though my jaw was wired and I couldn't talk. So it was really a one-way conversation.

Otis came to visit me whether I was conscious or unconscious. He'd pray for me, sing to me with his melodic baritone, and offer encouragements from the Bible. I was puzzled. Why would a busy man with an already hectic schedule use up precious time to sit with me? I told him one day, "Otis, you don't have to visit me every day. Surely you have more on your plate than coming to see me every day."

"I come to lift your spirits," he said. "You're the man who has encouraged so many hundreds, maybe even thousands, of people who needed encouragement and counsel or a word from God, before the car wreck stopped you." Otis paused and let his words settle in my mind. Then he said, "So I want to lift your spirits while you're here in the hospital."

Otis had previously accompanied me on trips overseas, providing music to complement my speaking. Often he had written songs that came from my sermons. Otis and his wife, Mervyl, a professional singer, often came together to the hospital to sing for me.

Even when I was sleeping or totally sedated, Otis and Mervyl always brought positive expressions through their songs. One of his own compositions was "Keep On Keeping On," which I recognized. Though I was probably sedated because of my wired jaw, even then I remember mustering up some control and movement of my hand. I started tapping the rhythm with my fingers.

No doubt I probably missed hearing some of their music when I was unconscious, but they cheered up Evie and any family members who came to see me too.

Many of the nurses and aides heard the songs, and they were touched by the contrast of my physical frailty compared with "the beautiful music of heaven" – as one nurse described it.

One night the First Free Church male chorus of about twenty men came to my floor and sang some songs for other patients and visitors. However, they also came into my room and sang a couple of songs. One of the songs was "He the Pearly Gates Will Open." I wasn't as blessed in hearing that one, wondering if they were asking the Lord to open the pearly gates for me to get in!

I'm not sure if I was coherent enough to sing along with them, but maybe I was tapping my fingertips on the side of my bed in time with the music.

* * *

There was another couple that frequently came to visit me – Denny and Evie Johnson. Denny was an effective businessman. His creative mind was always thinking of new possibilities and new ministries. He founded *Kids Around the World,* a nonprofit ministry, which as of 2016 has constructed more than 500 playgrounds in the United States and around the world. Evie and I have been members of that board.

There were a few other friends who also visited me almost

daily. One couple was Jeannie and Sam Mayo, both then pastors of First Assembly of God in Rockford.[8] Sam was senior pastor and Jeannie was the youth minister at their church.

As a fellow pastor, I know that ministers are always busy. Appointments, study, visitation, and administration keep pastors working long hours to get their work done. Here was a minister who came to pray, and he also took time to visit with Evie when I wasn't awake.

Pastor Mayo became a longtime friend, and after my recovery, we often met for lunch to exchange ideas and share God's blessings. On a radio conversation, Sam joked that I could have *any* face now. "You could've looked like a movie star or some other celebrity. Why not?"

However, Sam Mayo answered his own question. "I guess God probably said, 'I did such a good job on Lareau the first time. Why would you change it?'"

Our friendship had begun several years before my accident. We were two pastors with churches across the street from each other who came together to share our common church interests and concerns.

Sam Mayo and I began a long and God-blessed relationship of our two churches, and we even founded some joint church events. Our friendship was cemented even more firmly when Sam came to see me nearly every day I was in the hospital and rehab. For me, it had a tremendous impact.

John and Carol Evans were also prominent in my time in the hospital. From the initial time of my car accident and the subsequent prognosis that seemed so pessimistic, they began

---

[8] First Assembly of God in Rockford, Illinois, made a recent name change to Rockford First.

to do acts of selflessness. Carol got on the phone immediately to call friends and church families to ask them to pray for me.

John, as Barnabas board chairman, took a proactive step of making certain that Barnabas International would not suffer because of my absence from the office and the organization. John had to weigh heavy decisions in situations with the board and the Barnabas staff members.

Frank Nelson put in additional hours at the Barnabas office, making certain that funds were keeping pace with the ministry needs.

Tim Evans and his wife, Debbie, and their two preschool daughters started a daily prayer vigil for me and my family. Years later, when I was visiting my former church, Debbie introduced her now teenage daughters and told them, "This is Pastor Lareau Lindquist. He's the man who was in the bad accident in 1999, and we prayed for him during those months he was in the hospital and recovering."

I watched the girls' eyes widen, and together they said in a single voice, "Wow!" I saw a dramatic event that day – watching the girls understand the reality and power of prayer – *their prayers*.

I had to wonder how many other similar prayer vigils had taken place on my behalf. It was sobering that God was listening to countless voices asking essentially the same thing: *Please don't let Pastor Lindquist die.* Or, *Help Lareau, Lord, save his life and heal him.*

Upon hearing many such stories, I was overwhelmed by the outpouring of friends and people who didn't even know me. It made me grateful for every positive healing, or even setbacks, because I had learned that God can handle good as well as bad responses to my ordeal.

Indeed, *prayer makes a huge difference!*

Chapter Thirteen

Concern from Around the World

I was still not myself after several weeks in the hospital. My recovery was quite slow and much of my time was taken up with doctors and nurses. During those days, I wasn't totally aware of what was taking place in the hospital. The medications often affected certain areas of my brain, and my mind seemed to "check out" at various times.

It seemed to me that I had an environment of a hospital some of the time, and at other times I thought I was in the Radisson Hotel in Minneapolis. In the middle of the night, I'd look over my "hotel room" and wonder why another man was sharing the room.

In another version of dream-life, I was on a bus with friends from our Rockford Free Church and supposedly on our way to Minnesota. It seemed real to me, but I was confused because all the settings were different.

Occasionally when Rockford friends stopped by my hospital

room, I'd be halfway into their conversation, while my mind took me on a bus trip or to a hotel, church, or some other location.

Evie and I discussed those events, and she told me later, "I'm glad that you didn't have clarity then. I was grateful that your mind was confused, and your brain 'checked out' during the first week or two. If you'd had full knowledge of what happened, you might have been terribly frightened or depressed."

Evie wondered aloud if she was reflecting her own fears. "I suppose there were some times I 'lost it,' but then I'd see how many friends were praying for us and doing things for us. Overall, when something got bad, it never got worse. I think I didn't have many bad days. I'm so grateful that God helped me through most of the crises, but there were times ..."

I wouldn't have been surprised if Evie had such fears. She, of course, had taken the brunt of everything related to my car crash and injuries, and for those first few days, I was oblivious to it all. Evie had taken on a huge responsibility that I wasn't able to share with her. But by my reckoning, she took on her tasks with iron will and brilliance.

Her solidarity reminded me of Dr. Scott Nyquist, a member of my former church (First Evangelical Free Church in Rockford, Illinois) and a close friend. As a specialist in orthopedic medicine, he often stopped by my hospital room to check up on me, although he wasn't assigned as one of my doctors. Dr. Nyquist was active in the Free Church and led adult Sunday school classes. I always thought of him as an intelligent, godly man, but during my recovery, I was in *his* environment.

During one visit, I told him, "Doc, I'd like to tell you about my concern that Evie might get fears about my accident. Not only the crash, but about those early days and nights when I was out of touch with reality.

"When I became conscious again, I feared for Evie – that she might 'lose it' under the pressure and end up hospitalized herself. But she never collapsed or gave up.

"Evie handled all the critical decisions when I wasn't able to, while also calming our children and reassuring our grandchildren, plus soliciting prayers from our friends and ministry partners. Evie literally took over for us both."

Dr. Nyquist smiled. "Lareau, I've been stopping by to visit you whenever I can. You and Evie are both my friends, but let me tell you something."

"What's that?"

"I'm very familiar with hospitals and accidents. When someone's brought in like you were, it's often the spouse who takes care of matters while the victim, he or she, waits things out in the hospital. The patient gets the attention – treated by doctors, nurses, and others, but the spouse doesn't get any of that attention."

Dr. Nyquist paused, "In situations like that, the patient sleeps or is sedated, and the medical team sees to it that the patient avoids stress and concerns. The patient's spouse can't avoid the stress. That's what Evie has been doing for you, Lareau. Evie is your marriage partner, your children's parent, grandparent – even your stand-in for Barnabas. She signs and sends the checks, wrangles with the insurance company, makes other phone calls, consults with your doctors, and acts as your chief operating officer. Evie's doing all the jobs that need to be done while you heal."

Then Dr. Nyquist added, "When I come to my daily prayer list and see the name of Lindquist, I always pray for Evie first and you second, Lareau."

I still remember that conversation with Dr. Nyquist, and I see how true it is. Spouses bear the brunt of a trauma, accident, or sickness of the patient. They absorb the stress and fears, doing the work of two people, so the patient heals and begins getting strong.

I immediately could see how that happened in my situation. When Evie took charge of what I needed for my recovery, she was doing it as my wife and also as a nurse. More than that, she did so many other remarkable feats that probably took her beyond her expectations.

But she was up to the task. That gift from my dear wife is a debt that I'll never be able to repay.

* * *

It wasn't until some time later that I was able to get a sense of what had happened in my collision with a tree. Doctors wrote entries to my chart in the initial days of my hospitalization:[9]

DATE OF CONSULTATION: 01/22/1999

HISTORY: This 62-year-old gentleman is an unrestrained driver of a motor vehicle who either fell asleep or lost control of his vehicle, ran off the road, and struck a tree. He was attended by the paramedics at the scene. CPR was started. There was

---

9   Several chart entries were combined as a composite entry to eliminate duplication of information.

respiratory distress, and he was unresponsive and had a great deal of blood within the upper airway. He was intubated at the scene.

The patient was then brought here by paramedics and evaluated by two doctors. CAT scan of the head has been performed, showing what appears to be a small bleed, possibly in the third ventricle or the anterior circle of the Willis area. The ventricles are slightly enlarged. There are multiple facial fractures and sinuses, and with possible extension into the cribriform plate. No intracranial air is noted.

No subarachnoid bleed is noted.

Thoracic, lumbar, and cervical spine films reveal mild degenerative change but no obvious evidence of fractures, subluxations, or other abnormalities of the spine.

Thick bloody secretions have been suctioned from the endotracheal tube.

PHYSICAL EXAMINATION: Reveals this gentleman is intubated but awake. He is able to follow commands.

His pupils were visualized by emergency room physicians and found to be sluggish but reactive. His eyes are now swollen shut and can't be visualized.

No CSF (cerebral spinal fluid) was noted from the ears, nose, or mouth.

Multiple contusions, abrasions and bleeding are noted on the face. Motor exam reveals him to be able to move all four extremities grossly well with no gross weakness. Reflexes are hypoactive in the upper and lower extremities.

INDICATIONS: The driver likely absorbed great blunt force against his nasal and occipital frontal sockets, and he sustained major injury to his face.

ASSESSMENT:
    Concussion & closed head injury.
    Intra-cerebral hemorrhage.
    Multiple facial fractures.
    Severe facial swelling, with abrasions, lacerations, and an orotracheal tube is in place. No palpable crepitus.

PLAN: Observe from a neurosurgical standpoint and not perform an intra-cranial surgery at this point. Repeat CT scan would be reasonable in 48-72 hours or sooner if the patient deteriorates.

    With a pre-op diagnosis for facial fractures with complex naso-orbital- ethmoid fracture, with application of arch bars and intramaxillary fixation, the patient will be prepared for (plastic) surgery.

* * *

When a person's head receives great injuries, it also affects many other functions of the body. In my case, I suffered multiple fractures of nearly every part of my head. Think how many parts of the body the head controls, not just the many functions of the brain.

    The mouth serves as one of those singular features. It receives food and drink to nourish the body. It provides our tongue and

CONCERN FROM AROUND THE WORLD

taste buds, as well as saliva and teeth to grind food for chewing and swallowing.

The mouth also controls the sounds of our talking and singing, and provides other communication through expressions by moving the lips and muscles of the mouth. The mouth even allows breathing when the nose is broken or just stuffy.

The nose and sinuses are the first choice for breathing, filtering, and providing moisture for the air we breathe in and out, and sinus mucous is anti-microbial. The sinuses also provide our sense of smell, and to my comfort, my nose holds my eyeglasses on my face.

The broken facial bones caused numerous problems with my mouth, nose, jaw, cranium, and eye sockets. My eyes were affected seriously when my face was shattered, and particularly my eye sockets, as the trauma caused severe injuries to my eyes themselves.

Dr. Richard Coppeletti and Dr. Susan Fowell both examined my eyes. They both saw serious problems caused by the crash. Initially, the collision caused swelling so large that both eyes lost vision.

Once the swelling went down, there were issues with my eyeballs themselves. My left eye had lost vision completely, because the lens was injured. An artificial lens was implanted surgically, resulting in my eyes having issues with the retinas, followed later by double vision and a loss of depth perception.

During those early days, Dr. Fowell came to examine and treat my vision, which was difficult to assess due to my facial damage.

She explained, "The swelling makes it difficult to treat Mr.

Lindquist's vision. I believe he has double vision as a result of the accident. I may have to put the left eye 'to sleep' until some time later."

Dr. Fowell's calm explanation reassured me that I'd eventually regain my vision, though it might take time. But when Dr. Fowell decided to "put my left eye to sleep," she meant that by permanent dilation of the left eye to give me vision without double vision images.

There were other similar serious surgical adjustments to my jaw, my mouth, my nose, and just about every square inch of my face. To deal with my head injuries, the various doctors planned their strategies to deal with the most serious treatments first.

Ophthalmologists, internists, oral surgeons, pulmonologists, orthopedic surgeons, neurosurgeons, and plastic surgeons were called in. Once the various surgeries and treatments were done, there were other doctors who worked with my mouth, teeth, jaw, nose, eyes, spine, and knee. When repairing and restoring the bone structure of my head, there were plastic surgeons who tried to replicate the face I'd had all my life.

I also learned that they had to replace damaged bones in various parts of my face and skull. They sought out and harvested bone fragments from other parts of my body to graft into critical areas of my skull to make my face look like me. I recalled the pain and sensitivity of their harvesting of bone from my ilium (hip bone, part of the pelvis), and I also felt a great deal of pain during the healing of those places in my body.

Perhaps you remember the song "Dry Bones" that talks about bones in the body. Your toe bone's connected to your foot bone, along with the other connections of the bones. I often remember that song because I had bones taken from my hip and replaced onto my face: I say, "The hip bone's connected to the face bone."

People say, "Oh no, that's not the way it is."

I say, "Oh yes it is – that's the way it's in *my* body!"

A problem for the plastic surgeries for repairing my face included another problem for an oral surgeon (for my jaw). The problem was that my injuries were severe and my jaw was wired shut. Various doctors and surgeons collaborated to repair every area of my head and face.

To realign my jaw they had to break it. They started by cutting the jaw bones and adding other bone transplants from my hip to remake cheek bones and a missing nasal bone.

They replaced the bones around my eye sockets, restoring sinus cavities, adjusting the jaw, nose, and chin, all based on an overall plan.

Following all those surgeries, I had to start all over to learn how to use my new jaw for eating and swallowing. Those operations weren't life-threatening functions; rather they were more like new hindrances to get used to.

There were daily reminders that led me to accept that after those surgeries I felt that, "Things don't feel and work the same as they did before."

My first response after the bandages were removed from my face was that the surgeon did a great job. But Evie and I knew that it wasn't quite exactly the same face I used to have. We may have noted that change, but most other people didn't notice the slight differences – or perhaps they were too polite to point them out to me.

Evie and I accepted my facial surgeries as gifts from God, regardless of small differences. After all, I did get the face I had before, so we were greatly appreciative, even with the tiny flaws.

I had been in the hospital for many weeks and could have been bitter and frustrated for my confinement. In addition, for most of that time, I had my jaw wired shut. That meant I couldn't talk and couldn't chew and swallow my food. Eventually, after scores of meals of pureed food, Evie went to the GI (Gastro-Intestinal) doctor and asked, "Can't Lareau start eating regular food now?" At the time I couldn't pass a swallow test, but the doctor nevertheless okayed Evie's request.

Chapter Fourteen

The Paradox of Thorns

It took me at least a month before I could begin to sort it all out. During the time I was unconscious in the hospital those early days and weeks, I obviously didn't understand what was happening.

Even later when I was awake, those days and weeks were dulled with painkilling medication. Then when I came around, I had many questions and not many answers. Doctors had reservations about making direct prognoses, and they often waited with any long-term projections because of potential complications, changes in the recovery, or lack of progress with other various injuries.

Because of the uncertainties of my future recovery, Evie and I began considering options about the years ahead. Evie had to face the possibility I might not even survive the first night. The physicians believed that my prognosis was a 98 percent assurance *that I'd die.*

Thankfully, however, much later in my hospital stay, the physicians had turned the odds around. They offered me a more updated and positive outlook. The doctors told me that I'd have a recovery, but they all projected "some" years ahead for me.

I was often asked, "How are you doing, Lareau?"

Following my car wreck, I heard that question nearly every day when visitors came to see me. Over the months and fifteen years since and even today, I still hear that question: *How are you doing, Lareau?*

Considering the fact I had just a two percent chance of survival, I'm doing fine. Many doctors hedged, though, as some said that my long-term prognosis was uncertain – and *surviving?* All my physicians had to concede I had already done that.

While my doctors were positive about my survival in the short term, they reserved their prediction of the long term or any kind of open-ended prognosis. After all, there were still too many variables to assure me of a certain future, even though they indicated my basic health and repaired injuries could be good.

Then they opened my physical appointments by asking, "How are you *really* doing, Lareau?"

I'd remind them that I didn't lose the "bet" of a two percent chance of staying alive that cold January night, when they brought me into the hospital. I won that bet because of people praying and God's intervention. I took confidence by beating that earlier prognosis, and I really did stay alive during the first night and the next morning after the crash.

Ironically, doctors and friends still ask, "How are you *really* doing?"

With confidence and well-founded optimism, I'd respond,

"I'm doing well. In fact, I am *very* well." I had a habit of saying it with positive assurance, because I truly believed God to pull me through my dark incident – *and He did!* That opens my eyes to trusting Him.

Something remarkable took place during the next weeks in the hospital and rehab facility. I felt God showing me how to move forward in my slow and meticulous rehabilitation.

I drew from the Scriptures and discovered there were quite a number of examples of how God ministered to His chosen men and women. In the Old and New Testaments there are scores of incidents of His people contending against a number of crippling accidents, sickness, war casualties, leprosy, and evil oppression. Think of Job, Jonah, David, the apostles, Lazarus, and the Centurion's son.

I think of the man who was robbed and wounded on a highway on the way home. Jesus reminded us of that parable of the "Good Samaritan," who helped the man who otherwise would have been left to die.

And what about Jesus' mother, Mary. Think of her having to watch her son cruelly murdered on a rough cross. She must have had agonizing pain of her own, both physical, emotional, and mental. I believe Mary was overwhelmed by her terrifying and painful experience. Yet, I also believe God comforted her and healed her from her horror, grief, and worries about the future. Her appearances after the crucifixion that appear in the Bible show her in a status of peace and wellness.

As I thought of those examples of overcoming bad, perhaps even life-threatening events, I noticed that God healed those whom He wanted to help. Not everyone survives a "fatal" accident. Why?

Could it be the fact people prayed for my life as early as the crash itself? Or perhaps, the prayers of so many others prayed for me right after the accident? In fact, it amounted to literally hundreds, and by some accounts thousands, of people in the United States and overseas came together or individually prayed for me.

I do believe those prayers were major factors. I don't believe God makes some people lose their lives in tragic accidents while others survive. God is not capricious. He's a Sovereign God and His choices are always right.

I think often about how I was able to survive what was by all accounts a *fatal* collision. Yet I never totally discovered the *why* that the crash was intended for me. According to the best prognoses, the doctors were quite certain that I'd be dead before sunrise.

I've thought about this mystery often and how God, for reasons of His own allowed the crash as well as my recovery. Rather than brooding over the matter, I picked up wise words of the Scriptures. I decided that with God's help, I'd stop worrying about the future and start trusting.

However, sometimes a doctor or friend will ask, "Are there any continuing physical issues or problems that you still carry with you?"

My answer is always, "Yes. Every day I live with three reminders that still linger long after the collision." That's my way of pointing out I don't have the body I had before the crash.

Those lingering after effects are:

THE PARADOX OF THORNS

An issue with my left eye, when my eye surgeon deactivated the lens

A chewing and swallowing problem (dysphagia)

Continuing nasal and sinus deficits

These physical troubles are not life threatening for the most part, yet I took them to be my "thorn in the flesh." I was reminded that the apostle Paul had *a thorn in the flesh* that troubled him, and he asked God to take it away. It was some kind of unidentified troubling impediment, but it was so serious that Paul asked God to get rid of it for him.

Paul saw it as a hindrance and believed he'd be better off without it. So he prayed to God – three different times Paul asked God to take it away.

However, the Lord didn't respond to Paul's plea. True, God *could* take Paul's thorn away but instead gave Paul something better than removing it.

God told Paul that instead of taking away his problem, He would provide Paul with two attributes of His nature: *grace* and *strength*. He said to Paul, *My grace is sufficient for you, for my power is made perfect in weakness* (2 Corinthians 12:9 NIV).

It's apparent Paul had learned remarkable lessons from his thorn in the flesh. He not only accepted his difficulty – he went on to celebrate it as well.

Like the apostle Paul, I constantly latched on to similar threads of hope and prayed for healing. I felt that I was in limbo, not knowing what my future was. I wondered what God was really leading me to. It took me several years to sort through those physical paradoxes, and I have recently come to understand them more fully.

I've read many books, mainly biographies and other books that posed questions similar to my own questions. Three in particular have inspired me: Jerry Sittser's book *A Grace Disguised*; Don Piper's *90 Minutes in Heaven*; and one of the many great books of author C. S. Lewis, *A Grief Observed*.

I noticed over several years that these books reflect the experiences of their authors. Yet their stories show how God orchestrated bumps in the road in the lives of these Christians.

These authors also had to handle the fallout of the "wrecks" in their life experiences. I noticed that they eventually turned them around and found peace, comfort, and a remarkable blessing instead of despair that they initially encountered.

The stories of these authors, as the biblical examples stated above, have something in common. There are counterparts in God's Word where His children can overcome physical pain and suffering by seeking the healing of the spirit.

The human body heals by the medicine of the mind and soul. The body itself is the repository of the mind and soul, so that kind of healing requires God.

David didn't always cry out at his physical hurts; instead, he called out to God to heal his spirit and soul:

> *Whoever dwells in the shelter of the Most High will rest in the shadow of the Almighty. I will say of the LORD, "He is my refuge and my fortress, my God, in whom I trust." Surely he will save you from the fowler's snare and from the deadly pestilence. He will cover you with his feathers, and under his wings you will find refuge; his faithfulness will be your shield and rampart.*

You will not fear the terror of night, nor the arrow that flies by day, nor the pestilence that stalks in the darkness, nor the plague that destroys at midday. A thousand may fall at your side, ten thousand at your right hand, but it will not come near you. You will only observe with your eyes and see the punishment of the wicked. If you say, "The LORD is my refuge," and you make the Most High your dwelling, no harm will overtake you, no disaster will come near your tent. For he will command his angels concerning you to guard you in all your ways; they will lift you up in their hands, so that you will not strike your foot against a stone. You will tread on the lion and the cobra; you will trample the great lion and the serpent. "Because he loves me," says the LORD, "I will rescue him; I will protect him, for he acknowledges my name. He will call on me, and I will answer him; I will be with him in trouble, I will deliver him and honor him. With long life I will satisfy him and show him my salvation." (Psalm 91 NIV)

I've learned that not all my questions brought answers right away. It took me some time to appreciate all God did for me, and maybe even this is not a truly satisfactory answer. I will likely have to wait until I get to heaven to find out those answers.

That also brings back the three residual thorns of my accident: first, I have an issue with my left eye, because my eye surgeon deactivated the lens; second, I still have a chewing and swallowing problem; and third, I have continuing nasal and sinus deficits.

These reminders stick with me every day. As to my left eye, the lens was dislocated and so badly damaged the doctors had to surgically repair the left lens. My doctor also proposed to implant a special lens so that it might provide a clear image at the back of the eye where vision takes place. For two years following the accident, my doctors made numerous efforts to get my two eyes to work together, but the double vision never cleared. All I know is that the left lens doesn't work, leaving me with only the use of my right eye.

As to the second thorn, the doctors have tried to fix my chewing and swallowing problem, following my two facial restorative surgeries. The lower jaw didn't function following the surgery and still doesn't properly function to occlude with my upper jaw. The practical outcome of this makes me bite my tongue, cheek, or lips.

These frequent bites make it difficult for me to chew my food. It's even more difficult to swallow my food. Yet I believe that additional surgeries won't change that.

The third thorn that I am living with is a diminished functioning of nasal and sinus cavities due to their being crushed in the car crash. The doctors offered to try other surgical corrections, but they admit that in each of the three cases, they might not be successful.

Translation: they'd be experimental surgeries. I might be better off, or it could possibly be worse. With that uncertainty I decided, *Why risk it?*

I've also asked doctors about *their* opinion: "What should I do?"

Most of those surgeons said to me, "If I had that problem,

I'd probably do nothing. I'd leave those deficits as they are, since they're not life threatening."

I've agreed. In my case I can see benefits from my physical problems. After all, I'm alive, and I've come to consider those thorns as simple nuisances. I best identify with the apostle Paul when he spoke of the physical problem of his thorn in the flesh. Paul addresses this in his letter to the Corinthian church:

I was given a thorn in my flesh, a messenger of Satan, to torment me. Three times I pleaded with the Lord to take it away from me. But he said to me,

My grace is sufficient for you, for my power is made perfect in weakness.

Therefore I will boast all the more gladly about my weaknesses, so that Christ's power may rest on me. That is why, for Christ's sake, I delight in weaknesses, in insults, in hardships, in persecutions, in difficulties. For when I am weak, then I am strong.
(2 Corinthians 12:9-10 NIV)

There is often a paradox when someone receives a thorn, which can happen when he or she is confronted with a serious accident, injury, or disease.

When we ask God, "Why?" God doesn't always answer directly. But He may also show us why He allows some tragic event into our life – to show our loved ones His loving care and comfort family members if they lost their loved one through tragedy.

In both situations we see how a calamity can be turned into a great blessing that rises out of tragedy.

The apostle Paul learned a lifelong lesson that he shared in his letter to the Corinthians when he spoke of *his* physical thorn.

Thanks to God, I know now that my three physical thorns aren't life threatening, so I accept them. At worst, they're just a nuisance. I can wish that I didn't have those problems, but I think it's possible to live with a nuisance or two, or in my situation, three.

There are three other reminders of my car crash and its ongoing consequences. I presented them as three serious questions that I considered as spiritual thorns.

These are the three nagging questions that I prayed for God to show me answers to:

- Will I still have physical deficits?
- Will I able to continue my Barnabas ministry?
- Would my complications shorten my lifespan?

I don't yet have a complete answer for each question, but thanks to God, I've begun to accept His sovereign wisdom, and I'm comfortable in whatever God's answers turn out to be – for the thorns as well.

Chapter Fifteen

Thorns and Thrones

Others have even greater injuries and physical deficits – as in the case of Joni Eareckson Tada. Yet Joni, as did the apostle Paul, accepted the physical handicaps for the same reason Paul accepted his – to be drawn closer to God.

In her biography, Joni told readers that after diving into shallow water in Chesapeake Bay on July 30, 1967, she broke her neck.[10] That terrible injury could have cost Joni her life. Instead, it left her a quadriplegic with a prognosis of a short, dismal life span.

However, Joni had an amazing experience with God. She sought out God despite her physical deficits and got to know Him and love Him. Not long after her injury, Joni was interviewed by Barbara Walters on the *Today* show (NBC), and God used her tragedy to reach out to millions of people.

Joni's experience was one that helped me in my struggle

---

10 *Joni* by Joni Eareckson and Joe Musser, © 1976, Zondervan Publishing House. 2016 is the 40th anniversary of her book, which has sold more than 5 million copies.

through the contradictions and uncertainties of my accident and recovery. I met Joni when she came to speak at First Evangelical Free Church in Rockford, Illinois, when I was pastor. I remember a comment from that day when she said, "Oscar Wilde wrote: 'In this world there are only two tragedies. One is not getting what one wants – and the other is getting it.'"

Then Joni said, "To rephrase his thought, I suggest that there are likewise only two joys. One is having God answer all your prayers; the other is not receiving the answers to all your prayers. This is because I have found that God knows my needs infinitely better than I know them, and He is dependable, no matter which direction our circumstances take us."

I had read her book and met her when she spoke in my church. I remember her powerful testimony that day. I reread her book and saw how she handled her life during her dramatic injury and recuperation.

My own mental and spiritual wrestling began with questions surrounding the simple question, *Why did God allow the accident to happen?*

In her book Joni shared a number of rational reasons from God, answers from her prayers and the contradicting silence in response to her questions. Then she found spiritual answers for both reasons; they were found in God's Word and the books of godly men and women. In practical terms, she was able to see the hand of God handling *all of her suffering.*

How did that happen?

When she was a teenager, Joni was confronted with a major accident. She and her sister were taking advantage of the summer, swimming and lying in the sun on the beach with her friends. Joni said that she was resting on a floating wooden pier when she decided to dive into the Chesapeake Bay – but didn't notice the water was very shallow there. She was jolted at the bottom of her dive, hitting her head on the bottom of the bay.

Immediately she felt that she was caught in a net or some other trap, because she couldn't seem to move her limbs to lift her up and out of the water. Joni's collision with the bottom of the bay had broken her neck as well as fractured vertebrae that severed her spinal cord. She couldn't use her arms and legs. Fortunately, her sister Kathy rescued Joni before she drowned, dragged her to the beach, and called out for an ambulance.

God's plan for Joni included that near-death experience that took place in an instant, changing Joni's life forever and leaving her with the lifelong reality of quadriplegia.

After a long hospitalization and subsequent rehab, Joni learned how to cope with her deficits by painting and drawing artistic pictures, holding pens in her mouth to sketch fantastic artworks, or holding a paintbrushes to create water colors and oil portraits.

Would Joni have learned such lessons by avoiding that terrible dive into shallow water, which made her a quadriplegic? Joni doesn't think so. She has often said as much in her book and motion picture, *Joni*, as well as on her radio, TV, and print interviews and in subsequent books. She's often said she probably would have missed the whole point of God's "lessons" if not for her accident.

Later, she was led by God to study and reach millions of people through public speaking. She published her bestselling biography and played herself in a major motion picture based on her life story – followed up with dozens more books and television and radio broadcasts.[11]

Joni's career expanded when she founded Joni and Friends, a ministry dedicated to extending love and introducing Jesus Christ to people around the world who are affected by disabilities. God has had His hand on Joni's life for more than four decades now. But if Joni had never had that dramatic accident and its consequences, do you think her life might have been different?

She might've gone down the path other girls in her high school had taken. Like many other girls, Joni could've married a high school boyfriend, raised kids, and lived the rest of her life with that family. But God had other plans for her.

Like Joni's quadriplegia, sometimes a critical injury can become a benefit and a blessing. She learned God can turn a physical deficit into a powerful gift. He turns her helplessness into spiritual strength and power.

She has become a worldwide godly minister. Joni accepts her physical deficit, recognizing that God can turn troubles and problems into eternal assets.

Could I pray so my accident can also lead to ministry – one of encouraging and changing lives? After all, it is God who is truly our Adequacy.

As Paul told us to reach out to God as He reaches out and draws us to Him. We learn to know the Lord and love Him as never before. Paul says:

> *Don't worry about anything; instead, pray about everything; tell God your needs, and don't forget to*

---

[11] *Joni* was also a motion picture based on the Zondervan book and the movie was produced and distributed by *World Wide Pictures*.

thank him for his answers. If you do this, you will experience God's peace, which is far more wonderful than the human mind can understand. His peace will keep your thoughts and your hearts quiet and at rest as you trust in Christ Jesus. And now, brothers, as I close this letter, let me say this one more thing: Fix your thoughts on what is true and good and right. Think about things that are pure and lovely, and dwell on the fine, good things in others. Think about all you can praise God for and be glad about. Keep putting into practice all you learned from me and saw me doing, and the God of peace will be with you . . . for I can do everything God asks me to with the help of Christ who gives me the strength and power. (Philippians 4:6-9, 13 TLB)

Chapter Sixteen

God Is the Healer

In my early years when I attended Trinity College in Deerfield, just north of Chicago (before it became Trinity International University), our president, Dr. T. B. Madsen, was involved in a terrible automobile accident. It might have been a crash like mine in 1999.

Dr. Madsen was hospitalized for many months. I remember the student body had prayer vigils for his recovery, but the recovery did not have the medical advances of today that I was privileged to have.

Slowly he recovered from his injuries and finally returned to the college. When he spoke in chapel after his return, Dr. Madsen began his message with four simple words: "God has healed me."

As a young college student, I was surprised to hear him say that. I, along with the entire school body, knew that Dr. Madsen had undergone numerous treatments with hospital surgeons, nurses, and doctors. He had many surgeries, X-rays, medications, and medical tests, and a variety of then-modern medical procedures. Following all that, Dr. Madsen had to endure many weeks of rehabilitation.

Yet he said, "God has healed me."

At the time I thought that he should have mentioned all the medical treatments and equipment that seemed to be a part, or even the overall means, of the restoration of his injuries and health. As a young college student, I didn't even consider that God had healed Dr. Madsen. In my thinking, the medical team and hospital caused his recovery.

However, I didn't know what I have learned since then, when I had my crash and faced a serious, possibly fatal, outcome. Mine in 1999 had a similar perspective as Dr. Madsen's in the 1950s, almost fifty years later.

I don't recall if that college incident came to me while I was in the hospital after my crash. But my recent attitude is more like that of my college presidents. Yes, doctors, surgeons, and nurses have a major role in the recovery. Yet, ultimately, it is God who heals.

An incident that brings that into focus for me occurred when I was India, walking the streets of New Delhi. In the process of meeting some local Christians, I met an Indian medical doctor. He gave me one of his business cards. I politely took it and read the words on the card. The left side layout had two lines of words – one line mentioning the doctor's name and another line showing his medical and university degrees. But to the right side of the card were two balancing lines:

I Practice Medicine. God Heals People.

GOD IS THE HEALER

Too bad every doctor doesn't have the humility and realistic view of such life-death issues to recognize that God is really the Healer.

Yet if we recognize that God is our Healer, some person will counter that with another question: *How does He heal people?* I've gone to the Scriptures to look for that answer.

Here's some I've discovered:

A man in the Old Testament named Naaman had a serious disease. God told him to go to the river and dunk himself and he'd be healed. Naaman did as God told him, and he was healed. Yet there's only this one biblical reference to this method of dunking in the river for healing.

A man was simply identified as "the man born blind." Jesus made mud balls, pressed them on the man's eyelids, and he was healed. This shows Jesus healing in another way in the Bible.

A woman touched the hem of Jesus' garment, and she was cured of her blood disorder. By touching Jesus' garment for healing only occurred once, so it's not a preferred method of healing.

From the book of James, there is an instruction from God for healing that involved oil and prayer. That has continued to be a method of God's healing. It has continued over the years to be a vital method, but it is not the only method.

Is there a single answer to my earlier question? How does God heal? What is His preferred method?

My answer is this: God is not limited to any one method. His methods are varied. We can see the variety, and they are sometimes strange, such as sending someone to dunk himself in the river, or putting mud on blind eyes, or touching the hem of Jesus' robe.

Since God doesn't confine his healing to a specific method in the Bible, we have to take a look at what *He does*. The answer to that puzzle is that God is not limited to any one method to heal. He might use a surgeon to perform an operation, or he might not use a surgeon. He might use a prescription, or nothing at all.

God might heal a cancer with chemotherapy or radiation, or neither. He might use "something" or "nothing," but His methods are often inexplicable.

That's because He isn't limited to using any method or no method because it's *not the method at all* – it's God Himself who determines how he will heal a person. *He* is the Healer.

Back to the story. During my months in the hospital, there were all kinds of healing taking place. Some were operations, doctors' treatments, prescriptions, rehab, counseling, or therapy, and the works of all kinds of medical practitioners. All these were usually done independent of mystical biblical "methods" to heal people. There are scores, perhaps hundreds, of kinds of medical practitioners who do everything in their power to help injured or sick and bring healing.

They use a series of medical treatments even if they are done independent of God's direct presence or power. There are often surprises when patients, who were thought to be impossible to save, somehow stay alive and get better.

Doctors can claim the credit when that happens on their watch. I'm convinced that they sometimes have help when the prognosis is fatal, but someone recovers. That's when God has stepped in to help them. Many other Christian doctors that I've met also acknowledge that it's God who is the Healer.

When I was hospitalized during those months, I was overwhelmed with all the medical technology and the finest medical personnel with many treatments, sometimes many on any given day, and a large cadre of people who were part of that process. In a final analysis, I believe that *God healed me*.

Before I was even brought into the hospital on the night of my crash, there were a number of people contributing to my first aid, being in the right place at the right time to save my life. I could have died in the car but for the grace of God.

I believe that God had orchestrated all those "coincidence" factors for a greater concern. I'd be arrogant to believe that He did all that for me, alone. Early in my recovery, I thanked Him for keeping me alive and dealing with my injuries, so that I could continue my work. Yet, because of the various events during and following the crash and my hospitalization, God used those events to bring glory to Himself.

Chapter Seventeen

The Glory Factor

Not to us, LORD, not to us but to your name be the glory. (Psalm 115:1 NIV)

After the accident, and more specifically after my healing began, I found myself eagerly focusing on writing another book to stimulate my mind while my body continued to heal.[12] I had started on that book several years before my accident, based on a doctoral thesis on the same subject.

The project took quite a few years as I wanted to present new material on the subject – the glory of God. The book was to have two major sections: *What Is the Glory of God?* and *How Can I Bring Glory to God?*

I determined that very few people focus on that topic. My study has proven to me that many people don't understand

---

12 Lareau Lindquist's previous books: *Too Soon to Quit* published by Quadrus Media © 1994; *Why, Lord...Why?* published by Quadrus Media © 2007; *Glory, Glory, Glory* published by Xulon Press © 2010.

what the glory of God is all about. Yet, in my thinking there is no greater theme for the world than the glory of God.

We often use the expression as a flippant response to a situation or event, such as catching the green light to save a minute at the stop light, and someone humorously says, "Glory to God, I caught the green light!"

While such casual use of the expression seems almost irreverent to me, there are many people, even followers of Christ, who know very little about the topic. I did a great deal of study and research for that book, and when I asked people everywhere, "What is the glory of God?" this is what I discovered.

Most people will likely say, "I'm not sure what the glory of God means." So, after hearing the same innocuous replies, I felt determined to find biblical answers to the two earlier questions: (1) What Is the Glory of God? and (2) How Can I Bring Glory To God?

I thought it odd to hear people who never discussed the subject with me say that the glory of God was an important theme in the Bible, especially in the Psalms.

But beyond that, they didn't know what the glory of God meant. My quest took more than ten years and finally led to the completion and publishing of the book *Glory, Glory, Glory* in 2010.

I admit that during the earlier years of research and writing, I didn't have a good grasp of the theme either. I got deeply involved, and the theme of the glory of God became the basis of my doctoral studies.

Ironically, I found in the Scriptures that the word *glory*

appears in contexts of sickness, pain, suffering, fiery furnaces, and even the context of physical death.

Having spent many weeks in the hospital and rehabilitation, the one thing that I wished and prayed for was to get out of the hospital. I desperately wanted relief from pain, trouble, and loss – loss of many of the functions of my former body.

Doctors, nurses, and other medical people did their best to help me, but more than anything *I wanted my suffering to end.* I even began to rationalize that such a miracle could glorify God.

However, I became anxious. I wanted my suffering to end so much that it became a fixation, and my thoughts always were on those themes.

Then, in my study for the book on God's glory, I found verses in John 12 that opened my eyes. Jesus prayed, "Now my soul is troubled, and what shall I say? *"Father, save me from this hour"? No, it was for this very reason I came to this hour. Father, glorify your name!* (John 12:27-28 NIV).

I was truly startled to read that. I thought about Jesus' human body. His humanity meant He faced pain, suffering, and the ultimate death of crucifixion. He no doubt would have preferred, humanly, to bypass what was ahead for Him on the cross. It was the second half of the text that stopped me in my tracks.

Take a look at those verses. First Jesus called upon God to save Him from pain, suffering, and death, but Jesus' deity also figured into the equation. His humanity wanted relief from the torturous hours ahead.

Another thought came instantly to His mind. He knew that He had come to do what God was demanding of His Son, so

Jesus acknowledged the Father's mandate and said, *No, it was for this very reason I came to this hour. Father, glorify your name!*

Thinking about that shift from His humanity to His deity is too distant from our human minds to comprehend. Still, there is something rich and meaningful for us to emulate.

Our first thought is to skirt around the tough stuff, to bypass the hurt, fear, suffering, pain, and even death. If we have a choice, we'd all choose to take that road that takes us away from real troubles. We want relief from pain and death – who wouldn't?

We need to go to a higher plane where God hears our prayers echoing Jesus: *Father, glorify Your name.*

There have been many times in my hospitalization and even later that I wanted to get out of the hospital and get out of my pain and suffering. I'd usually ask, as Jesus did, for God to "save me from this hour."

Eventually, I became fixated on the second thought of Jesus that modified the first thought. Instead of longing for release from pain, He longed for the Father to be glorified, and He called out a second thought: *Father, glorify Your name.*

Pause for a minute. Think about what's going on in your life. Is it physical or psychic (mental) pain? It could be a financial pressure or strife and discord in your home or family. Perhaps it's a sickness or injury that is causing fear, stress, pain, or threat of death.

It's natural for humans to seek relief. However, could you respond the way Jesus did? First, He called on God to save Him. Then He weighed His suffering against what God had already asked Him to do. He responded, *No, it was for this very reason I came to this hour. Father, glorify your name!*

I mentioned earlier that when I was in the hospital, I often asked God for relief from pain and for healing. However, I found an illustration in John 12 that turned around my fears and frustrations. I followed the example of Jesus and did what Jesus did, namely what God wanted Him to do: *His mandate was to do the Father's will.*

I believe that Jesus also has a mandate for us. He expects us to offer our lives to glorify God. I think there's an important consideration for us:

If any of you wants to serve me, then follow me. Then you'll be where I am, ready to serve at a moment's notice. The Father will honor and reward anyone who serves me. (John 12:26 MSG)

If we have committed our lives to Christ and are serving Him, it's our assignment, whether we have wonderful health or are in a hospital trying to achieve freedom from pain or recovery from illness or injury, to focus on the better thought, "Father, glorify Your name, no matter what is going on in my life right now." Our circumstances don't impede what God wants us to do for Him.

As in the case of Joni Eareckson Tada or any other believers who have serious troubles, it is possible to glorify God, even in the toughest times of life.

I was in the hospital pleading for God to help me get back my strength, health, vision, and all the other deficits I "owned" as the result of my accident. I learned over many weeks that the worst times for me were the best times, because those were the times I was close to God. In my effort to receive recovery,

I learned that doing the will of God was really what I wanted and what He wanted.

Even now, in your toughest hours, God is ready to bring something good out of your mess. He might remove your obstacle, or He might give you strength to use your life for Him, even if He doesn't remove the obstacle or threat.

Chapter Eighteen

The Miracle Man

After being released from my hospitalization about eleven weeks after the crash, I made a visit to one of my favorite restaurants in Rockford. It was a treat to be out of the hospital and the rehab facility. It felt good to be returning to some sense of normalcy. We ran into several people we knew at the restaurant, as we always had before, but it was especially refreshing to have them greet Evie and me. After months of no Swedish pancakes, we gulped them down with zest.

After our meal a man came up to us where we were sitting. He looked familiar, but I couldn't think of his name. (I had some memory lapses, and Evie had to prompt me about the people coming our way.) In this case Evie whispered, "I think this guy's a member of First Free Church."

The man introduced himself, "Hi, Pastor Lindquist. I'm Bob Ellison. I'm so pleased to see you up and around. The last time I saw you was at the site of your wreck in January."

"You were *there*?" I asked, surprised.

"Yes. There was a nurse inside the car caring for you even before the fire ambulance came to the scene. She kept you alive. I heard her say on her cell phone to the hospital that you had life-threatening injuries. After they took you away in the ambulance, I had no idea it was you, and so I went home. My home is just a mile from your crash."

"That's amazing that you were so close to me."

Bob nodded. "After they took you to the hospital, I went home, pulled my GMC pickup into my driveway and prayed, even before I got out of the pickup. I prayed that you'd stay alive. I was convinced when they took you away that you might not make it, so I prayed more seriously that you'd stay alive. Like Jesus said, *Pray without ceasing*."

I thanked Bob and told him, "I'm convinced it was you and so many others' prayers that saved my life."

Bob nodded and then added, "It was amazing! When I went to church on Sunday, they told us that you were the guy in the crash, and I had watched you leave by ambulance, but I didn't even recognize you."

We chatted a few more minutes, and I thanked Bob again for his prayers for my recovery. Then after he left us and left the restaurant, we went to the cashier's counter to pay our check. The cashier looked up and recognized me. She took my credit card and the meal check and said, "How is the 'miracle man'?"

I smiled, but said, "Let me tell you about the Miracle Man."

"Oh, good. All of us here want to hear the details."

"*I'm* not the Miracle Man. I'm a *miracle recipient*."

The cashier looked a bit disappointed and suddenly had a

facial expression that seemed to say, "How'd I ever get myself into this?"

I didn't want to hurt her feelings and sent a prayer heavenward, thinking fast to know what to say. "I'm sorry," I said to her. "It's just that I don't consider myself a miracle man. You see, the real Miracle Man is Jesus. He's the one who *creates* our miracles."

The cashier smiled. She liked what she heard. "I believe you're right, Pastor." She gazed her eyes upward and nodded. "Yes, Jesus is the Miracle Man for certain."

That incident was what I like to call a teaching moment. On the way out of the restaurant still thinking about the "Miracle Man" discussion, I remembered from the book of Acts that it was the apostle Peter who confirmed that Jesus was the Miracle Man.

In Acts chapters 3 and 4, the author Luke gives great detail of an amazing story about Peter's declaration to his listeners that Jesus, the Son of God, was the Miracle Man.

Peter's story and mine have striking similarities.

Please excuse the apparent arrogance of my comparing myself with the apostle Peter – I'm just proof of Peter's point. It also offers a comparison for you as well. It's likely that you could find the same discovery in your life as I did in mine. It has to do with your relationship with Jesus Christ.

Luke tells the story of Peter and John going to the temple for daily afternoon prayers. As they were approaching the entrance of the temple, they were met with a crippled man. The man held out his hand, asking for money.

Peter told the man, "I don't have money, but I have something better." The beggar must have been surprised at Peter's response—*Silver or gold I do not have, but what I do have I give you. In the name of Jesus Christ of Nazareth, walk!* (Acts 3:6 NIV). Peter took the beggar's right hand and pulled him up. Immediately the man's feet and ankles became strong enough to stand. Then he tentatively began to walk. Moments later bystanders were watching him – amazed that he was walking, running, and jumping up and down, praising God.

Everyone recognized that this was the beggar who sat daily at the temple gate. They knew him as a beggar who'd been out there "forever." Luke observed that the crowd was, *filled with wonder and amazement* (Acts 3:10 NIV).

More than that, Luke described the pandemonium, as the apostle Peter saw the crowds' astonishment. Peter addressed them:

> *Oh, Israelites, why does this take you by such complete surprise, and why stare at us as if our power or piety made him walk? The God of Abraham and Isaac and Jacob, the God of our ancestors, has glorified his Son Jesus. The very One that Pilate called innocent, you repudiated. You repudiated the Holy One, the Just One, and asked for a murderer in his place. You no sooner killed the Author of Life than God raised him from the dead—and we're the witnesses. Faith in Jesus' name put this man, whose condition you know so well, on his feet—yes, faith and nothing but faith put this man healed and whole right before your eyes.*
>
> *And now, friends, I know you had no idea what you*

were doing when you killed Jesus, and neither did your leaders. But God, who through the preaching of all the prophets had said all along that his Messiah would be killed, knew exactly what you were doing and used it to fulfill his plans.

Now it's time to change your ways! Turn to face God so he can wipe away your sins, pour out showers of blessing to refresh you, and send you the Messiah he prepared for you, namely, Jesus. For the time being he must remain out of sight in heaven until everything is restored to order again just the way God, through the preaching of his holy prophets of old, said it would be. (Acts 3:12b-21 MSG)

It's interesting to hear Peter refuse to take credit for something that God had done. Earlier in his discipleship with Jesus, he was the proud egotist of the twelve disciples much of the time. Several times in the Gospels, Peter took the spotlight and even asked Jesus if he would be sitting beside Him when the Lord ascended to His throne.

Peter's brusque braggadocio was arrogant and self-serving, and the night before Jesus was crucified, it was Peter who denied Jesus. However, now he was hardly the same man. He had changed.

As Peter addressed the crowd outside the temple, he wasn't the old Peter. Now he was honest about himself and knew that it wasn't he who created the miracle of giving the beggar the ability to walk.

No, Peter wasn't the Miracle Man. He didn't take credit for

the healing. It was Jesus who performed the miracle of healing the crippled beggar.

Instead of taking that credit, Peter instead pointed to Jesus as the Miracle Man, and he directed the crowd to seek out Jesus, saying to them:

> *It's time to change your ways! Turn to God—not me—because God sent you the Messiah. Jesus, the Messiah, was the one you and your leaders killed. It's by the Name of Jesus Christ of Nazareth that this man you remember as the beggar who couldn't walk is now jumping and dancing because of his miracle of healing.*[13]

I can relate to Peter, as I recall that story in the book of Acts. When I read that story, I was sobered by how someone thought of me as a "miracle man." No, not me.

It's been fifteen years since my nearly fatal car crash. During those years, I have often been asked questions by friends and those who heard about it in some of my speaking engagements or in conversations when it came up as a story of how God works.

Write a book? I didn't rush out to do it. I had to think about it over and over for at least a decade.

Initially I refused to write such a book because I was afraid if I did, it'd focus on me and that bothered me. A book about me? I told Evie and close friends that I chose not to push my near-death experience into the limelight as if I were some kind of celebrity.

Instead, it was after that conversation with the cashier at the restaurant. Her casual comment of me being a miracle man

---

[13] Paraphrased from *The Message*, © 2002.

really made me think. I decided I didn't want to have such a story written unless God gets the glory, not me.

I also prayed about it and talked to several key people whom I trust and who know me. They all agreed with me that I should exclude self-promotion as the focus of the book. Instead, it should bring glory to God. That's exactly what I prayed before starting the book.

So I find myself again reminding people that I am not the Miracle Man in this story. I prayed that the focus should be on Jesus. It's too easy for us to take credit for something we didn't do. God did the miracle, and we are just recipients of His grace. That's why I don't try to grab the limelight.

Sometimes I point to the doctors and nurses. They were truly important in saving my life, despite the initial prognosis that offered virtually no hope.

In another vein, I point out how nurse Kristin Dolphin kept me breathing and my heart beating. I included Kristin in those earlier chapters, because she pointed out that *it was God who kept me alive* – perhaps by orchestrating events to culminate at the right place and time. Kristin didn't see them as so many coincidences, especially when she later saw how "miracles" were linked to my injuries and recovery.

Some people who were on site that fateful night on Alpine Road were probably not attuned to seeing God at work. Yet some did see the Lord taking over that accident site.

There were also many people who were in the hospital later to care for me. They could have taken credit for keeping me alive and guiding through recovery. Most of them will tell you that they were in the ER or hospital rooms, "Just doing my job."

As I look back on my experiences, I believe that the talents and gifts of people were dramatically used by God not just to help me stay alive and able to continue my ministry. I also believe that God used my situation to make an impact on a vast number of people, perhaps including a handful at the accident site who acknowledged that God had His hand on me and my surprising outcome.

There were other people, some who knew me before and after the accident, who sensed that God was significantly behind my miraculous recovery. I have seen crowds of people at speaking engagements, and I see them from the pulpit as I speak. I see in their faces that they understand that my experience wasn't something that I did, but they recognize that it was of God.

The same is true of the thousands of people from all around the world who were touched by a supernatural pull to pray for me and then saw their prayers answered in remarkable ways.

Jesus – the Great Physician – is the real Miracle Man.

Chapter Nineteen

Is God Ever Too Late?

We tend to think of time in minutes, hours, days, weeks, months, and years. We wear wristwatches. We have clocks and calendars in our homes, cars, and offices, as well as on our cell phones. You and I live within the limitations of time and space. We are busy. We continually rush here and there.

How different it is with God. I can't imagine Him looking at the clock. He is never late, and He is never too early. God is always on time. His timing is always perfect.

I recall the story of Mary and Martha (John 11) who were frantically trying to reach Jesus so He could come and heal their sick brother, Lazarus. Jesus eventually arrived, but according to the two sisters, He was late – too late by their timetable.

Lazarus was dead. The Bible goes on to describe that he was truly dead – not in a coma or unconscious state. John pointed out that Lazarus had lain in the tomb for four days. The tomb held the stench of death. Mary and Martha both said to Jesus, "If only you would have been here."

You know the rest of the story. Jesus walked toward the entrance of the tomb and called out to Lazarus to come out of the gravesite. Amazingly, Lazarus did, still wrapped in his burial shroud.

That day the sisters learned something quite new about Jesus. They saw Him perform the miracle of a resurrection of a human who had died, and He gave Lazarus a renewal of his life, as referenced in John 11:25. Jesus wasn't late at all!

Is God ever late? No, He is never too late. He is always there at the right time, though sometimes it seems to us that He is too late. We wring our hands, wishing and praying for God to do something – now!

God is always doing something. We don't always know it, but He's aware of our troubles and is fully engaged in our serious problems, accidents, tragedies, and our other "hurts." *He is there!*

At the time of my near-death automobile accident, especially during my unconscious state, God came to me and did a number of remarkable things to reveal Himself and His power.

Looking back, I see them as miracles.

You've just read my story, but I want to underscore some afterthoughts in this chapter. Please consider the lessons I learned from my experience of avoiding death, my recovery, and the repair of my physical injuries during my doubt-ridden dark days.

By seeing how God orchestrated the details and sequences of my near-death event, you might see how I have learned those lessons. Yes, I had to experience those events the hard way, but they were used lovingly and efficiently by God to heal me and to bless me.

That doesn't seem possible? Could a loving God have prevented my accident? Of course, He could. Yet, looking back I've had time to "rewind" those events, and I've found too many amazing "coincidences" that I cited in the previous chapter. There were many more.

For instance, I was awake before the collision, because apparently I lowered the car windows before the crash – probably to blow cold air on my face to keep me awake.

In other chapters, you've read how Kristin Dolphin, a local nurse, miraculously arrived at the scene even before the fire department paramedics and ambulance. Kristin's initial evaluation of the wreck she saw on the site convinced her that she had to take charge of things until paramedics arrived.

The doors of my wrecked car were jammed. As a trained nurse, she swiftly got herself to the victim. Though the jammed car doors failed, she took advantage of the two open car windows. She climbed inside through the passenger window to reach me and began CPR to keep my lungs breathing and my heart beating.

That divine timing and other miraculous aspects literally saved my life until the fire department first responders and the ambulance arrived on the scene. Even though some of them determined that my situation seemed fatal, believing my injuries were too severe to fix, they nevertheless put themselves to work to do everything in their capacity to keep me alive.

God's preparation and timing were more than perfect

coincidences. There were so many incredible events that they couldn't be unusual odds or luck.

Too many coincidences in the series of events would be off the chart of mathematical probability. All these actions, laid out in necessary sequence with split-second timing, challenge any notions that such events could happen by coincidence:

My car crossed three or four lanes of busy traffic without hitting another vehicle or killing or hurting other drivers or passengers.

Kristin came upon the site within minutes, or even seconds, after the crash – before the EMTs, ambulance, and firemen.

Rita was in the car with Kristin to care for Kristin's baby while she helped me stay alive.

A bystander was by the open window of the driver's side, who encouraged me to keep breathing while Kristin was calling 911.

The fire department wanted to use the Jaws of Life, but Kristin discouraged them. There was no time. So a paramedic climbed through the car window to untangle me and lift me into the ambulance.

Miraculously, the hospital was only two miles away, so the ambulance got me there in moments.

In the hospital, after the emergency treatments, my coma was a way that God could help my brain and body deal with the trauma that otherwise might have taken my life.

God was there at the right time and place. He was present at the crash site, then went with me to the hospital, and was present throughout my three-month recovery.

I believe the events of that night were more than a sequence of coincidences. God timed each miraculous phenomenon

– who, what, where, when, why, and how – with His guidance and presence.

This doesn't diminish the efforts of the people at the scene who, with God's help, kept me alive. Their presence was critical, keeping me alive long enough to get me to the hospital and for the doctors to take over in the emergency room.

Over the weeks, I had often cried out, *How long, Lord* – through surgeries, therapies, rehabilitation, and various complications that continued week after miserable week. In contrast to my misery, weeks later I got a clear picture of how God guided the critical moments of those first efforts by the ones who came to my rescue. These events showed me God's overriding involvement in our lives.

Kristin also told Evie and me that she no longer uses phrases like, "Things just happen," or "That guy got a lucky break," "Count your lucky stars," and other similar insipid remarks.

She added, "I'm convinced that a sovereign God had already arranged my schedule that night. He put me in the right place at the right time."

I too had time to reflect on God's perfect timing as it fits into my situation. It reminds me of Galatians 4:4: *When the fullness of time had come, God sent forth His Son* (NKJV).

Stated a bit differently, we can say, "When the time was right," or "When God had all things in readiness, He sent forth His Son." That means that the birth of Jesus was *perfectly timed*.

Remarkably, so are the events in your life and mine! Incredibly, God's omnipresence and His omniscient concern are made real in "accidents" such as mine.

Most of the time we aren't conscious of God's involvement

in our lives. Sometimes we're amazed to see what God does after He does it. In such situations, as Barnabas International Director Perry Bradford often points out such events as, "It's a 'God thing.'" That may sound colloquial, but it's true. We must give the glory to God.

God is the great architect of the universe – but also of our lives – yours and mine. Trust God as you are in His presence, even if you don't "feel like it." When we are overwhelmed, we must turn to God at once. Wait upon Him and His plans for you. Then, when you've shared your thoughts with Him, you will find yourself being encouraged.

My favorite two words, *Be encouraged,* are the valediction sign-off of my monthly *Encouragement* letter. I sometimes also use this verse from David's experience in the Old Testament when he reminds us, *Remember the wonders He has done,* [and] *His miracles* (Psalm 105:5 NIV).

As David admonished the people of Israel to remember the wonders and miracles that the Lord had already done, he calls people *to remember the wonders and miracles* that God already *has done* for you – along with those miracles that we joyfully anticipate. God is faithful to bring *wonders and miracles* to you at just the right time.

When I was critically injured in that automobile accident in 1999, I praised God that I hadn't died. Now I can continue to praise God that He has kept me alive. After weeks of hospitalization – first in a coma; then with a jaw wired shut, unable to talk or eat; and strapped in my hospital bed, unable to walk – I can now do all of those things.

Friends and medical experts agree that God did a remarkable

thing for me, and He is still doing great things in and to *me*, and giving me a future ministry.

These have been multiple wonders and, without hesitation, using the word David used in Psalm 105:5 – *miracles*. The word is absolutely appropriate.

One of the encouragements that I received was music. It's almost as inspiring to me as the Scriptures, such as these three encouragement verses from John Newton's hymn "Amazing Grace":

> 'Twas Grace that taught my heart to fear,
> And Grace, my fears relieved;
> How precious did that Grace appear,
> The hour I first believed!
>
> Through many dangers, toils, and snares,
> I have already come;
> 'Tis Grace hath brought me safe thus far,
> And Grace will lead me home.
>
> The Lord has promised good to me,
> His word my hope secures;
> He will my shield and portion be
> As long as life endures.

I found peace and recovery, and I discovered in my journey that God had never abandoned me. Many wrote me, saying something like this: *Lareau, you have encouraged me faithfully through the years. Now it's my turn to encourage you.* They let me know that he or she would pray for Evie and me.

I have felt the love and the power of people's prayers. Receiving encouragement from so many, I hope that other revivals of prayer and encouragement might sweep though our churches and our ministries around the world. As Paul so frequently wrote *Encourage one another* (Hebrews 3:13 NIV).

In our many trips to scores of countries, we've seen even many more such remarkable *wonders and miracles* over the past thirty years. We continue to pray for more revivals, more answers to prayer, and plenty more of Christian encouragement.

> *There are so many other things Jesus did. If they were all written down, each of them, one by one, I can't imagine a world big enough to hold such a library of books.* (John 21:25 MSG)

Be Encouraged!

Photos

Inside what's left of Lareau's Pontiac

The crashed Pontiac

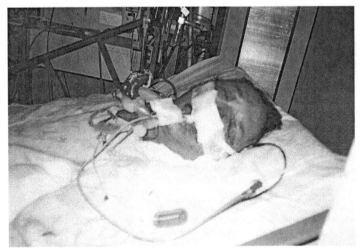

In the hospital

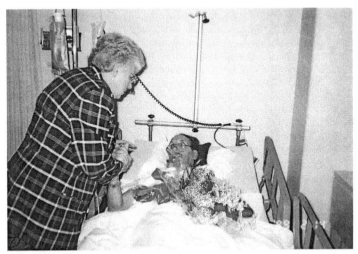

Evie with Lareau

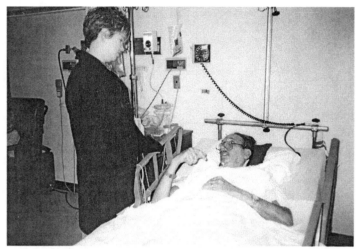

Kristin with Lareau

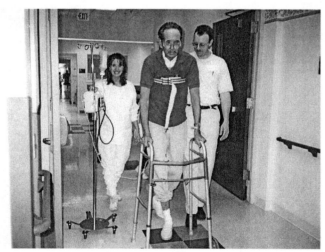

Learning to walk

One year anniversary at the accident scene

Lareau with Kristin at the accident scene

Lareau and Evie Lindquist Information

Contacts:

Barnabas International
431 South Phelps Avenue • Rockford, IL 61108
Or Write: P.O. Box 11211 • Rockford, IL 61126

Telephone: (815) 395-1335

E-mail: barnabas@barnabas.org

Barnabas International Website: www.barnabas.org

Encouragement Letters:
https://www.barnabas.org/letters.php

Meet the Author

DR. LAREAU LINDQUIST has had a career as a pastor in churches in Nebraska, Minnesota, California, and Illinois, along with his wife Evelyn (Evie). In 1986 Lareau and Evie Lindquist had a two week assignment with Wycliffe Bible Translators in South America. While there they saw the positive results of their assignment, and they made a decision to start an ongoing ministry of encouragement with assignments in other countries of the world. That concept led to their founding of Barnabas International, now in its 28th year of ministry. Lareau Lindquist is an international speaker and author of several published books.

Often disguised as something that would help him, evil accompanies Christian on his journey to the Celestial City. As you walk with him, you'll begin to identify today's many religious pitfalls. These are presented by men such as Pliable, who turns back at the Slough of Despond; and Ignorance, who believes he's a true follower of Christ when he's really only trusting in himself. Each character represented in this allegory is intentionally and profoundly accurate in its depiction of what we see all around us, and unfortunately, what we too often see in ourselves. But while Christian is injured and nearly killed, he eventually prevails to the end. So can you.

The best part of this book is the Bible verses added to the text. The original Pilgrim's Progress listed the Bible verse references, but the verses themselves are so impactful when tied to the scenes in this allegory, that they are now included within the text of this book. The text is tweaked just enough to make it readable today, for the young and the old. Youngsters in particular will be drawn to the original illustrations included in this wonderful classic.

Available where books are sold

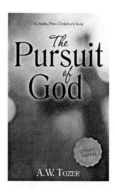

To have found God and still to pursue Him is a paradox of love, scorned indeed by the too-easily-satisfied religious person, but justified in happy experience by the children of the burning heart. Saint Bernard of Clairvaux stated this holy paradox in a musical four-line poem that will be instantly understood by every worshipping soul:

> *We taste Thee, O Thou Living Bread,*
> *And long to feast upon Thee still:*
> *We drink of Thee, the Fountainhead*
> *And thirst our souls from Thee to fill.*

Come near to the holy men and women of the past and you will soon feel the heat of their desire after God. Let A. W. Tozer's pursuit of God spur you also into a genuine hunger and thirst to truly know God.

Available where books are sold

CPSIA information can be obtained
at www.ICGtesting.com
Printed in the USA
FFOW05n1115171116